P9-DET-620

Retiring?

RETIRING?

Your Next Chapter Is about
__Much__ More Than Money

TED KAUFMAN
and
BRUCE HILAND

HOUNDSTOOTH
PRESS

COPYRIGHT © 2021 TED KAUFMAN & BRUCE HILAND

All rights reserved.

RETIRING?

Your Next Chapter Is about Much More Than Money

ISBN   978-1-5445-1683-7 *Paperback*
       978-1-5445-1684-4 *Ebook*

To Ginny and Lynne and our wonderful families.

CONTENTS

100 percent of the profits from this book will be donated to charity.

I

WHAT'S THE PROBLEM?

"It is better to live rich than to die rich."

—SAMUEL JOHNSON

Why this book? We both had satisfying careers working alongside accomplished professionals, officials, executives, and entrepreneurs, and we're fortunate today to be enjoying happy, fulfilling retirements. Four years ago, we were comparing experiences and discovered how many friends, acquaintances, and former colleagues were *unhappy* in their retirements. As we shared observations and anecdotes, we were surprised at the problems many of them experienced. They didn't seem to be financial problems; instead, it appeared that their unhappiness stemmed from other issues.

We explored further and discovered that while they had all done the financial planning for a *materially* secure retirement, they had paid scant, if any, attention to the major life changes that come with retirement. Intrigued by this, we listened to and talked with dozens of retirees about their experiences moving from their careers into the *terra incognita* of retirement. They all agreed financial planning was a prerequisite but also agreed—

many emphatically—that realizing a successful retirement requires equal if not more attention to nonfinancial issues.

As we reflected on what we'd learned, two messages came through loud and clear:

- First, retirement has changed enormously in the last few decades in its duration, the circumstances giving rise to it, and decisions the individual has to make.
- Second, most of those we spoke to were unprepared for the profound personal and life changes retirement brings. Addressing these nonfinancial issues seemed to hold the key to a satisfying and fulfilling retirement, but only financial matters had gotten the necessary attention.

We were curious about what was going on, and we both agreed we wanted to try to help. And then Ted said, "You know, we ought to write a book." So we did.

We've put together this concise and, we hope, practical guide for the individual approaching retirement or perhaps for the recent retiree now confronting the challenges we describe. We hope to help you by framing the important questions and pointing you in helpful directions. Clearly, our perspective is shaped by the scope of our careers, our retired lives, and, importantly, by our age and gender. We'll readily acknowledge that, try as we might, we can't fully appreciate how different a woman's experience may be nor how someone twenty years younger than us may see their choices and the challenges. We certainly don't present ourselves as authorities. Indeed, *you* are the authority for creating *your* retirement.

Now let's get to work.

For too many people approaching retirement, only financial planning has gotten the necessary attention. Whether they've overlooked, ignored, or avoided the nonfinancial challenges, they risk being unprepared for the profound personal and life changes that retirement brings. A few real-life examples make the point:

- A financial-services executive had been retired for a year. She had done little preparation other than financial planning and was repeatedly waking in the middle of the night worrying, "What am I going to do? What can I do? This is a disaster! Maybe I should go back to work."
- A public employee said, "My best friends for years have been the people I worked with every day. Once I retired, I found we didn't have much to talk about beyond business. After several lunches without the business issues to talk about, we drifted apart."
- An attorney was consumed by his career and had no other interests, hobbies, or plans. He fought his firm's mandatory retirement policy right up to his last day at the office.
- At a cocktail party, a recently retired hospital CEO complained ceaselessly about his first six months in retirement. He was bored. He had nothing to do. His complaints went on and on.
- A corporate executive who'd retired at sixty-five planned on spending his days playing golf and poker with the guys at the country club. At age seventy, he developed several physical problems that inhibited his golf game. He could still play but knew his game was deteriorating, and he was no longer competitive with his friends. He decided to give up the game.

How does this happen? People approaching retirement tend to get their financial planning done for several reasons: the benefits are obvious, so much help is readily available, and the wealth-management industry spends tens of millions on advertising. As well, hundreds of books, workshops, and seminars are available. Why haven't these same smart, successful people paid serious attention to the nonfinancial dimensions of retirement?

Perhaps because most approaching retirement have practically no real-world experience with what people actually *do* after they retire, not to mention how their lives change. Their parents' retirement experience is outdated for several reasons we'll explore. They know little about how retirees actually live day-to-day or what issues they face other than the general fact of aging. They don't have much to go on.

As they approach retirement, they may still be so consumed by their job that they have little time or energy to really think about it. Often their most intense, demanding work years are the three to five years leading up to retirement, which leaves little time, space, or energy to contemplate retirement's realities.

According to one prominent wealth manager and seconded by an experienced psychotherapist, *denial* is a more likely explanation. Denial is that unconscious psychological defense mechanism people have for avoiding a problem or issue. Why would otherwise thoughtful, prudent individuals not address these important nonfinancial issues? Because paying attention to fears, feelings, and relationships can be uncomfortable. And planning what is truly the next chapter of your life without a roadmap can seem daunting. Coming to grips with the specifics of retired life and the uncertainties of growing older is challenging and can be stressful and even a bit scary. Bottom line: many otherwise prudent and capable individuals avoid coming to grips with the nonfinancial issues altogether.

Despite all these factors, we were surprised by how eager people were to talk about the problems they'd experienced and the insights they'd gained. We concluded that, for complex reasons, people rationalize *not* addressing those nonfinancial issues but recognize they *should*. Further, they encouraged us to take on the challenge of writing this book. One said, "It's really important you're doing that. That stuff is every bit as important as the money side, maybe more so." Another said, "Wow, what you guys are doing is really, really needed. I want copies to give to some friends and relatives as soon as it's printed."

That framed the question: what would be the most effective way to help people approaching retirement deal with these important nonfinancial decisions? The effort involved in doing a good job is not a trivial task. They'll need to examine their habits and behaviors and think deeply about personal values, relationships, and life goals.

What's the best way to help? Obviously, every individual's retirement will be unique, so that rules out an "owner's manual" approach. Everyone has distinct interests, needs, expectations, and limitations; that eliminates the cookbook approach. However, a number of *successfully* retired people we talked with described dealing with retirement as a "journey." They described their retired life as a "new adventure." Aha! Something akin to travel—so we've structured this as a guidebook to help you plan the next chapter of your life, to think through this extraordinarily important journey: finding and enjoying a satisfying, meaningful life when you retire.

You know from experience that when you organize an important trip, you have lots of questions: where to go, when to go, how to travel, where to stay, what to see, what to skip, etc. Each traveler answers those questions differently based on their own resources, expectations, and preferences. To help you plan *your* journey into and through your next chapter, we will pose questions, help with some context, and offer suggestions and resources. But, for your journey to be a success, it is entirely up to you to shape your answers and capture your preferences, priorities, and expectations.

We've made two assumptions about you.

- First, we've assumed your goal is to make the next chapter of your life satisfying, enjoyable, and meaningful. This goal deserves the same clear thinking and hard work you applied in your career and to important life decisions. To reach your goal, you will need to address a broad range of issues to develop a plan that will yield you the freedom and purpose you've earned.
- Second, we've assumed you've done your financial planning or, at a minimum, have it well underway. Just as the starting point for a trip is determining what you can afford, it's essential you understand your financial resources as you work out your answers. If not, get to work on that task immediately.

A few caveats before we start. This work is not something you can do quickly. You certainly can't just sit down at your desk and work through it start to finish. The process we will describe is fluid, nonlinear, and heuristic. That means that once you get to work, you'll find yourself moving back and forth. As you deal with a particular idea or come up with useful information, you may find that idea or information could change from something you've considered earlier. This book has wide margins and worksheets for notes, and a notebook or your smartphone's Notes app should be a constant companion. Thoughts and questions will pop up, and it's wise to capture them as they occur. When you happen upon interesting ideas and would like to know more, get in the habit of looking things up. Google is your helper.

Here's how we'll move ahead. We start by describing the changes that accompany retirement. They are probably much more significant than you expect. Then we move to the questions you'll need to answer. The big questions include "When to retire?", "What will I do?", and "Where will I/we live?" Then we will ask you to think about how you will care for your body, your brain, your heart, and your soul, or, said differently, your physical, intellectual, emotional, and spiritual well-being.

You'll find there are very few quick answers. Some questions will be comfortable and others less so. Each merits your best thinking. While you may feel comfortable dealing with some issues on your own, we—and *everyone* we've talked to—believe that input from others is critical, starting with your partner, the term we use throughout the book to refer to your spouse, partner, or significant other. One approach is asking your partner to complete the exercises and worksheets in parallel with your efforts. (Note: additional copies of worksheets and exercises can be printed from our website http://retiringyourlife.com/.) Sharing answers can facilitate important discussions and improve your planning.

Similarly, give some careful thought as to how you want to include close family members and friends. It will help to explain clearly that you're systematically and carefully considering the consequences of your retirement. (You could give them a copy of this book!) Open communication as to what you're doing and how you're doing it should help avoid misunderstandings and facilitate their participation.

If you can talk with people who retired some time ago, you may find they faced similar challenges and opportunities; their guidance can really help as well. Remember, there's neither a need to nor reward for reinventing the wheel.

Our guidebook approach recognizes that although others have trod similar paths, your retirement experience—like your vacation trip—will be yours alone. Your answers will be entirely personal as they must be to shape a plan that works for you. Consequently, we avoid prescriptive advice wherever we can and instead offer suggestions and relay others' relevant experiences. As well, there is an abundance of accessible literature on virtually every subject you'll consider. *Whenever you see a numbered notation in the text, that means that you can look in Appendix A and find a suggested book, article, or website with helpful information.* To make your life easier, all the references and resources are also listed on the book's website at http://retiringyourlife.com/.

If you're ready to work, let's go. If not, you might consider lending this book to someone you know who is ready to use it.

II

RETIREMENT HAS CHANGED...
WHAT TO EXPECT

"Change is great. You go first."

Over the past few decades, retirement has fundamentally changed, so much so that when we started writing this book, we searched hard for another word to use. Retirement as a word and concept still carries historical baggage, conjuring up a cartoon image: the gold watch presented for "your long and loyal service to Acme, Inc." Then off to the golf course for ten years. Then gone. Today that version of retirement is inaccurate and—worse—irrelevant. Retirement today begins the next chapter of your life.

The American retirement landscape has changed dramatically. Consider:

- The 401(k) largely displaced the guaranteed-income pension plan.
- When you retire now tends to be an individual choice as opposed to a policy based on your age.

- People are living longer. Medical advances and increased attention to physical fitness have lengthened how long you'll be retired. The *average* sixty-five year old today has a life expectancy of twenty years. Those with better education and above-average income tend to live even longer. This means that if you retire between fifty-five and sixty-five, your next chapter may last more than thirty years.
- The onset of age-related health problems has slowed. This means more of those thirty-plus years will likely be active and healthy.
- A career with a single employer is now virtually unheard of. Today the average American planning for retirement will have spent only four years in any one job.
- Ageism is alive and well, especially in the tech field. We've heard many stories of successful executives being shunted to the side because they're "old."

The implications of these changes extend far beyond the impact on your financial planning. The new retirement is no longer when you receive your gold watch and pension. It *is* when you can begin working for yourself and controlling your own schedule. Your planning needs to focus on how you want to *live* the next chapter of your life. Those added years mean the chapter is a full-length chapter, and retirement is truly a new life experience. That shift requires a different mindset, and this task deserves your best and most serious attention. It's a much greater challenge than in the gold watch days. (See Appendix A, resource II-1.)

These changes in work environments and life expectancy allow for greater variability in how and when people retire. The decision to retire increasingly involves personal choice. More people now partially retire. It's no longer unusual to see some people deciding to retire in their fifties. In contrast, others choose to work well into their seventies. Whenever they choose to leave their career work, today's retiree is likely to be physically and mentally fit. Thus, they may seek demanding activities, ones that require hard work and thought. Technology-driven services have expanded opportunities and, in turn, choices. Hardware and software now can make any place effectively an office. In many locations—not just the larger cities—fully equipped offices are available for rent by the hour, day, or week. You no longer need an office or staff to be involved in complex activities. Communication capabilities are ubiquitous, enabling you to stay in touch 24/7 most anywhere you are.

Even with so many more choices—or perhaps because of them—very few have paid enough attention to the scope and complexity of shaping and constructing the next phase of their lives. Clearly, retirement today is much more than playing golf, watching TV, reading a good book in a hammock, taking long walks with grandchildren, or, as the frustrated spouse dealing with an aimless new retiree observed, rearranging the spice shelf.

As earlier noted, there are plenty of rationalizations for putting off serious attention to retirement. In your early fifties, you likely were in full-powered pursuit of success. A few years later, retirement might've seemed a distant sanctuary promising relief from stressful fifty- to sixty-hour workweeks. For too many, it's only when the date is in clear sight that any preparation starts.

First comes financial planning, which can be reasonably comfortable. It's fact-based and rational, and help is readily available. That work often prompts getting legalities in order, developing an estate plan, and updating wills. Again, for those tasks, professional help is readily available and usually involves only a few meetings. Working on financial and estate plans may evoke dreams about exotic escapes and start conversations with your partner about "what we want to do when we retire." Too often, however, those subjects get put aside as something to be "talked about later" or added to the clichéd bucket list. Far too often, financial and estate planning add up to the beginning and end of retirement planning.

Now the purpose—yours and ours—is to consider the *rest* of the picture. When you retire, you'll experience profound changes in your life. Some are positive, and you very likely look forward to when

- You no longer have to dance to anyone else's tune. You'll be free to choose and explore your own daily rhythms.
- You set your own goals, define your own performance targets, and decide what you'll do and when you'll do it.
- You have control of your time—daily, weekly, monthly, and beyond.
- You can pursue great adventures and whims, try new things, and rediscover forgotten pleasures.
- You have quality time for your partner, your family, and friends.

But the transition from work to retirement can be jarring as the changes triggered by retirement will very likely upset your equilibrium, perhaps dramatically. These changes stem from leaving your work life's structure, relationships, satisfactions, and support systems. While some may resemble other challenges you've faced along the way, the *aggregate* impact of these changes can be enormous. Failure to take these changes into account is a formula for failure.

As with other important life events you may have experienced—major job changes, relocations, divorce—a successful transition involves many personal changes. Some you will feel quickly, others more slowly. But the changes will occur, and they will be significant. Virtually everyone finds it stressful, since you find yourself treading new ground.

We describe these changes as profound. Here's why:

- The rhythm of your life will change. In your work life it's likely that only the weekend buffers your week's hyperactive pace. Your workday also likely dictates when you wake and when you go to bed. Your annual calendar probably has tightly defined periods for vacation and holidays. All these aspects of your routine—determining your daily, weekly, monthly, and annual life rhythms—are up for redefinition.
- Your very identity will change. Your role, position, and status in most of your relationships will be redefined. In the workplace, your position establishes your status with commensurate respect and privileges. With retirement, you become a "formerly" or "used-to-be." As well, outside the workplace—in your community, for instance—your position shapes your status and others' perception of you. That's up for change, too. (II-1)
- Most of your work relationships center on the work you do. When that common connection goes away, many of those relationships will fade, some immediately and others more slowly. Social interaction is essential to your health and well-being, but the opportunities to interact with others change significantly.
- The tasks you complete create personal satisfaction and a sense of accomplishment. When those tasks go away, so do those opportunities for positive reinforcement.

- You may have enjoyed a support system that helped manage your time, travel, and many daily tasks; that will go away. You immediately become your own personal assistant, travel department, and social secretary.
- You'll have less structure. Most of us became acclimated to the work-driven structure with meeting schedules, trips, tasks, and deadlines. When that structure goes away, your choices multiply. You can—indeed, you must—choose what to do and when to do it.
- The context of your life will change—geographically, situationally, and emotionally. You'll no longer need to reside close to your workplace. Your personal contacts, points of attention, and most daily experiences will change.

Dealing with changes on this scale can, even for the strongest individual, trigger a fight-or-flight response. But neither fight nor flight is an option. There's simply no way around it: your life will be significantly different after you retire. While the specific changes men and women face upon retirement differ somewhat, the magnitude of the challenges does not. (II-2)

Your choice then is to either embrace the challenge of dealing with a new reality or indulge in denial (i.e., plunging ahead as if nothing is going to change). So many of the unhappy retirement stories we heard were the fruits of denial. You don't want to go there.

Embracing change involves hard work and presents new challenges. The breadth and depth of changes you'll face offer a compelling argument for serious planning. However, we understand that for some, the mere mention of planning sets off alarms. Planning may feel too much like work. During your career you may have seen planning efforts consume valuable time and energy but yield very little. And we'll concede there's an element of truth in the historic military cliché "Every plan is a good one—until the first shot is fired." Mike Tyson's contemporary version is even more vivid: "Everyone has a plan until they get punched in the mouth." That said, the planning we're encouraging and spelling out in this book is solely intended to get you to answer a few important questions. Again, our only objective is to help you improve the chances for you to have a satisfying, fulfilling retirement. And there's no report to write.

There's one final reason for this planning: it provides a certain insurance value when reality intrudes. What do we mean by "... when reality intrudes?" We mean that sudden, unplanned event that turns your world upside down. Or it may be not so sudden. It could be a loved one's death, a turn for the worse in your or a loved one's physical or mental health. It could be a fire, a hurricane, or that proverbial "bolt out of the blue"—anything that disrupts your world. The thoughts, discussions, and decisions you work through in this guidebook will provide you with a solid foundation for the decisions you'll have to make as you adjust to a new reality.

Over the past three years, we've asked retirees across several socioeconomic levels to talk about their experience entering retirement and activities that helped them adjust. As you'd expect, no single activity worked for everyone, but an interesting pattern emerged. There seem to be three stages of retirement:

- **Transition**—from day one through the first few years. This is when you'll be applying the work you'll be doing with this guidebook and finding your new rhythm.
- **Real Retirement**—follows and lasts until you have to make significant changes to accommodate issues that come with aging. We hope that will be many years.

- **Seniority**—when you have to make major adjustments to handle the realities of aging.

Our principle focus in this book is to help you get ready for your transition. This is when you'll be building your successful retirement. If you get the first few years right, you'll improve your chances to enjoy a long, satisfying, and meaningful retirement.

To recap: retiring involves withdrawing from many of the relationships and support systems that were central elements to your work life. How this impacts you will vary, but changes will occur. For many, work demands that they adjust their lives in order to accommodate their jobs' demands. Work determines what you do and how you do it, both at the office and in your personal life. Your job is more than just a source of income. In many ways, it defines you. Separating from those relationships, as well as the structure and support your work environment offers, is a life transformation worth serious attention, which is why you're doing this planning.

Among the reasons you've been successful is that you've learned how to anticipate and adapt to change. The magnitude of adjustments accompanying retirement can be unsettling, but, fortunately, not all happen at the same time. You'll have more choices than ever before. This is good news if you've done your planning. It can be bad news if you haven't. So let's get on with it.

III

GETTING STARTED

"Those who plan do better than those who do not plan even though they rarely stick to their plan."

—WINSTON CHURCHILL

Your answers to three interconnected questions will provide your planning architecture: When will you retire? What do you want to do? Where should you live? How are those questions interconnected? Your answer to one question may shape or change your answers to others. For example, you might want your retirement date to enable you to pursue a teaching opportunity, which in turn might involve relocating. All three questions will require certainly some if not considerable research and thorough discussion. Each leads to making a major decision and warrants your and your partner's best, unhurried thinking.

As you'd do before a tennis match or a run, it's a good idea to stretch and loosen up first, in this case the mind rather than the muscles. Two mental exercises will help stimulate your imagination, provoke reflection, and get you thinking "outside the nine dots." As you work, try to keep in mind how retirement will change your life's rhythm. It's likely you've run full speed in your work life. Now try to imagine having total control over how you'll spend your time and freedom to make choices in a wholly different way. One great pleasure of retirement is, in fact, you *can* stop and smell the roses. It's easier said than done, but take it from us: finding your new rhythm is well worth the effort. With that in mind, let's get started.

We want to get you thinking as broadly as possible about what *you* want to do with *your* newly available time and freedom when you retire. The first exercise involves making a list of what you value most in life. Wow! Clearly, this is not a trivial question, and it's one that deserves continuing thought and regular updating. Even on the first try, it may be helpful to do several drafts. Start off by jotting down four to six ideas about what you value most in life. You don't have to rank them; just get something down on paper or on your computer. Some people identify relationships such as loved ones, family members, and friends. Others think of experiences they associate with deep happiness or freedom, such as fishing in a quiet stream, a view from a mountaintop, or a quiet hour in a great cathedral. Some value how others perceive them—powerful, kind, trustworthy, or loyal. Others value tangible items, such as their home or an art collection. If you have a partner, it might be helpful to ask him/her to do this exercise at the same time. There are no right or correct answers, only *your* answers.

WHAT I VALUE

....

....

....

....

....

....

....

....

....

....

....

....

....

....

....

....

The second exercise involves making a list of things you *never* want to do again. For instance, many leaving organizational life often mention sitting in pointless meetings or dealing with petty personality conflicts. Many mention being overscheduled. Some don't want anyone telling them what to do. Others identify people they don't want to reencounter, and some name places they never want to return to. As you work on this list, also make notes as to *why* you feel what you feel. It's interesting how assessing why you *don't* like something, someplace, or somebody can help you clarify what *does* appeal to you. This list, too, is worth revisiting from time to time.

NEVER AGAIN   **WHY**

....

....

....

....

....

....

....

....

....

....

....

....

....

....

Now that your mind is properly stretched and loosened up, we can move on to the first question. While there is no particularly correct sequence for addressing these three questions, deciding when to retire seems the least complex task, so we'll start there. As you work through this question, keep in mind that your answer will be your best *initial* estimate as to when you want to retire.

You might be asking yourself, "How do I determine the best time to retire?" Daily life offers signals that can help you recognize when it might be time to step away. Some of the feelings listed below may be familiar from other times when you considered changing jobs. None by itself is definitive. The worksheet may help you rank and weigh the various considerations. Doing so will help you form a hypothesis as to when you wish to retire. Here are some indicators:

- You feel the stress level of your job is excessive (III-1, 2)
  - ☐ Strongly agree
  - ☐ Agree
  - ☐ Not an issue
  - ☐ Disagree
  - ☐ Strongly disagree

- You're concerned about your health
  - ☐ Strongly agree
  - ☐ Agree
  - ☐ Not an issue
  - ☐ Disagree
  - ☐ Strongly disagree

- You're no longer finding satisfaction in your work
  - ☐ Strongly agree
  - ☐ Agree
  - ☐ Not an issue
  - ☐ Disagree
  - ☐ Strongly disagree

- Aspects of your job you've always found exciting now bore you
  - ☐ Strongly agree
  - ☐ Agree
  - ☐ Not an issue
  - ☐ Disagree
  - ☐ Strongly disagree

- You're fed up with interpersonal and/or administrative problems
  - ☐ Strongly agree
  - ☐ Agree
  - ☐ Not an issue
  - ☐ Disagree
  - ☐ Strongly disagree

- You're tired of working for someone else
  - ☐ Strongly agree
  - ☐ Agree
  - ☐ Not an issue
  - ☐ Disagree
  - ☐ Strongly disagree

- You want to control your schedule
  - ☐ Strongly agree
  - ☐ Agree
  - ☐ Not an issue
  - ☐ Disagree
  - ☐ Strongly disagree

- You want a much more flexible work schedule
  - ☐ Strongly agree
  - ☐ Agree
  - ☐ Not an issue
  - ☐ Disagree
  - ☐ Strongly disagree

- You have specific things you want to do while you're physically and mentally able
  - ☐ Strongly agree
  - ☐ Agree
  - ☐ Not an issue
  - ☐ Disagree
  - ☐ Strongly disagree

- You have an opportunity to do something completely different—an offer to teach, to join a colleague in a joint venture, to write a book
  - ☐ Strongly agree
  - ☐ Agree
  - ☐ Not an issue
  - ☐ Disagree
  - ☐ Strongly disagree

- You want to spend more and better time with family and good friends
  - ☐ Strongly agree
  - ☐ Agree
  - ☐ Not an issue
  - ☐ Disagree
  - ☐ Strongly disagree

A university president found himself frequently up at night worrying about the many challenges of his job. His partner grew concerned about stress-related illnesses and helped him realize his job was taxing his health. They decided, like a student uncertain about entering college, to take a "gap year" and come up with a plan for the rest of their lives.

Another factor deserves mentioning. It's what social scientist Arthur Brooks, writing in *The Atlantic Monthly,* called the complex challenge of "professional decline." That is, the sense you're no longer performing at the top of your game and the impact this has on your happiness. He notes that some high achievers struggle to find replacement activities that afford them an adequate measure of relevance. (III-3)

One story illustrates how anticipating this issue can help. A lawyer friend explained how his sports experience helped him plan the timing of his retirement, shape his retirement plan, and make the transition from career to new activities. As well as being a successful attorney, he'd been a talented and serious amateur basketball player, first or second scorer for his team. As he aged and his skills began to decline, he discovered he still enjoyed being the third, then fourth, and eventually the fifth scorer. As retirement approached, he drew on that experience and systematically ratcheted back his lawyering in his firm. That exit strategy helped him continue to enjoy his work life but also allowed him to take on other activities as he transitioned into retirement.

Back to the question of when. Once again we remind you to involve your partner (if appropriate) as soon as you seriously start considering your options. If you have two careers, then the challenge is even greater. Whether or not your partner is employed, retirement will change your shared day-to-day reality. If your partner has a career, the challenge becomes even more complex. The complications of synchronizing two retirements can be tricky, and some find that involving a professional as a sounding board and counselor helps greatly. You'll find that hearing yourself describe your issues and concerns to another person will clarify your thinking. And the questions an objective outsider poses will help clarify priorities and alternatives. (III-4)

For some, the answer to *when* may seem relatively simple if your employer has a policy requiring retirement at a certain date. But that policy simply defines your *latest* retirement date. In the financial-planning process, your advisors should identify the financial consequences of retiring at various ages. As you give serious attention to what you want to do after retiring—the question we'll address next—you may well discover you want to leave earlier than you'd thought. One corporate executive's story offers a vivid example.

> A good friend and colleague started working on me in my early fifties to plan for retirement at sixty. He explained that by working until sixty-five, I'd lose five of the best years of life. As he put it, "things start to fall off at seventy." He was absolutely right.

Absent the dictates of a policy, you might want to retire after sixty-five. That would be a decision informed by what you want to be doing after you retire. Your financial planning helps define your options, and, while retiring earlier may be attractive, you might have very good reasons to put retirement off.

If you're fortunate enough to love your work, which some will argue means it isn't "work," then you can design an approach to gradually reduce your workload.

With the loosening of retirement policies, the options for "soft "retirements have increased, most commonly via a planned reduction in hours and days worked and shedding specific responsibilities.

When you settle on a date, think of it as a hypothesis you'll test as you move on to the more challenging question of what you want to do, which is perhaps the most consequential question and likely the toughest.

IV

————

WHAT DO YOU WANT TO DO?

"You've got to be very careful if you don't know where you're going, because you might not get there."

—YOGI BERRA

As the philosopher cited above points out, deciding what you want to do is a very important question. It is complex—perhaps the toughest and most important of the three. A senior partner at a distinguished Wall Street firm summed up the challenge this way: "You must—repeat must!—have another serious, consuming interest before you make the move."

In conversation after conversation, we've found that asking people what they *want* to do frequently elicits that deer-in-headlights expression. Identifying or discovering that interest—or interests—will require your best thinking and dedicated time. Ideally, you should start figuring out what you want to do concurrently with your financial planning.

As a reference point, here are two approaches to retirement planning that *don't* work:

- One entrepreneur dismissively—and somewhat defensively—defined his retirement plan as "working four days a week." That may sound like a workable *partial* retirement, but it left unanswered what he'll do on that fifth day, and the sixth and seventh. Simply put, that's not a retirement plan. Most people we know who tried that approach slipped back into working full time and admit they've never gotten around to doing the things they said they wanted to do.
- A *Wall Street Journal* letter to the editor captured another approach. The writer dismissed the advice he'd gotten about retirement and asserted that "…long walks, good books, and playing with grandchildren…" would keep him happy and fulfilled. That might have worked a few decades ago when retirements were shorter, but that plan won't suffice for twenty or thirty years. Realistically, solitary pursuits like long walks and reading can get old fast; grandchildren have busy, full lives; and, as we'll discuss later, the failure to stay engaged with others is unhealthy.

Deciding what to do is a—perhaps *the*—key question. Where to start? A successful and happily retired real estate developer suggests you plan your next chapter the way he developed a shopping mall. The first question a mall developer faces is "What will be the anchor store?" Everything else follows from this decision, because the anchor store will be the major factor in the mall's success. Successful retirees similarly have an anchor—perhaps two—that lets them confidently answer the question they're frequently asked: "What are you doing?"

Your anchor is limited only by your imagination and circumstances—teaching, writing, starting a business, exploring a new talent, or fully developing one you already have, such as art, gardening, or photography. You may have more than a single activity. Two is not uncommon, but three seems to be pushing it. The core idea is to define your anchor so you can fit other interesting, satisfying activities around it, like filling in the smaller stores in the mall.

It may be obvious but still needs to be said: the odds are that golf or any other recreational sport will not be a lifetime activity. For example, no matter how much you love golf, playing every day can lose its appeal and a reality intrusion such as a bad back, hip, knee, or shoulder can abruptly end or severely limit your participation.

Before we plunge into the broad sweep of your options, we want you to consider your first few months of retirement. Not surprisingly, many want to take a complete break upon retiring. The desire may be to rest and refuel or to indulge as you've never done before—explore the countryside on a motorcycle, live for three months in Paris, go to cooking school, see Antarctica, or travel the Silk Road. If you and your partner conclude taking time off is a good idea, then go ahead and do it. *But* it's *not* a good idea if you don't have a plan ready upon your return. We've heard too many stories about unprepared retirees suffering reentry shock once they find their weeks are empty and their calendars blank.

That you're reading this book means you're fortunate enough to be considering what you *want* to do. The odds are you've pursued your career's work with such focus and energy that you've given little thought to how you'll spend your time and energy when that work ends. Working hard is a good thing, and there is ample research confirming that work can provide meaning in your life. Moreover, recent research indicates that the need to find meaning in your life increases after you turn sixty. Retirement provides the opportunity to reflect on what you've done and how you've done it, which highlights how important it is to have serious, consuming interests when you retire.

As you approach this question, it's important to realize how remarkably broad your options are. (IV-1) Over the last three years, we've talked to retirees at various socioeconomic levels asking them to discuss the activities that worked to make their retirement successful. Naturally, no activities worked for everyone, but we hope the scope of their experiences will help as you create your retirement plan. Appendix C offers an extensive list of activities that retirees told us worked for them.

It's also worth noting that in the course of those conversations, several activities were specifically discouraged:

- Day trading in stocks, bonds, precious metals, and bitcoins. Their advice is to leave that to the professionals. Similarly, sports gambling, casinos, and lottery games.
- Spending hours on Facebook, Twitter, and other social media. Sure, check in on family members and friends, but they are no substitute for human contact.
- Sitting around watching TV all day.
- Eating or drinking to excess.

And while it seems amazing to still have to even mention it, they did:

- Stop smoking!!!

Additionally, they identified a few common leisure activities that were worthwhile but cautioned they be done *in moderation*, not at the expense of time spent with others:

- Reading
- Catching up on movies and TV
- Corresponding via email and social media
- Walking the dog and/or getting a cat

One keen observer summed it up this way: "If you stay in your pajamas, you die."

Enough negatives. Creating a list of your possible anchors is easier than you might think. You may have started already—if not on paper then in the back of your mind. As you begin, ask yourself how you might use your accumulated skills and wisdom. Along the way you've accumulated a lifetime of experiences and knowledge, which might be valuable to others if you're willing to share it. It's well worth spending the time to compile a list of your skills, knowledge, and expertise. The cumulative worth of your experiences is easy to undervalue. Consider the African proverb "When an elder dies, a library burns down." We expect you will be surprised how much ends up on your page.

SKILLS

....

....

....

....

KNOWLEDGE

....

....

....

....

EXPERIENCE

....

....

....

....

Here are a few questions to stimulate your thinking about how you might invest your time:

- Are you interested in continuing educational programs? What subjects?
- Are there subject areas in which you have sufficient expertise to consult, teach, or coach? At what level?
- Do you want to contribute your skills and energy to your community? How do you define your community? Would you like to volunteer? Hold elected office?
- How much time can you imagine yourself spending on the arts (e.g., painting, music, theater, literature)? As a participant or supporter?
- Are you interested in helping entrepreneurs? As an angel investor? Or by mentoring?
- Are you interested in serving on corporate or charitable organization boards? Are you interested in philanthropy?
- Do you want to work around animals? Coach a children's athletic team? Work in a retail job?

Don't be surprised to find yourself considering things that are very far from your work life. They might bring you real satisfaction and fulfillment. Consider these examples:

- A highly regarded psychotherapist retired from counseling powerful movers and shakers in Washington, DC, and is now volunteering and leading book discussions at her community's elderly services center.
- A Wall Street executive in his mid-seventies is happily dividing his time between working at an animal rescue shelter and coaching an eighth-grade girls' lacrosse team.
- Before he retired, a corporate attorney with a serious lifelong interest in wine asked the proprietor of his local wine store

about a sales job. The surprised owner didn't have an opening, so the attorney offered to work for free until someone left. He now has a job doing something he loves and quite enjoys the double takes from former colleagues finding him behind the counter.

An overview of broad categories of activities may help structure your thinking.

TRAVEL

Most have travel at or near the top of their lists of things to do in retirement: places you've never been, locations briefly visited on business trips, or too-brief visits without time to fully enjoy them. As you consider your choices, keep in mind the physical demands and the limitations resulting from the pandemic. Adventure travel is most satisfying when you can participate fully. Later, comfortable cruises offer their own rewards. Although some retirees travel in their eighties (and even nineties!), travel comfort decreases with physical impairments, as does your tolerance for the hassle of dealing with air, rail, and car travel.

SPORTS AND GAMES

Like travel, sports and games are a mainstay of many early retirement plans. The activities covered a broad range, including individually competitive sports (golf, tennis), team sports (crewing on a ship), and coaching. Like travel, sports-related activities tend to fit best into your early retirement years when your physical conditioning and energy tend to be the highest.

EDUCATION

Continuing or lifelong education has grown dramatically. Years ago, people might have moved to a college or university town to access institutional resources. Today, educational opportunities are almost everywhere, either in person or on the internet.

THE ARTS

The arts provide an extraordinary array of rewarding retirement activities. Examples include performing in orchestras, choirs, or bands; dance; drama; folk art; writing; painting; sculpture; photography; craft arts; television; radio; film; video; and sound recording.

MONEY-MAKING ACTIVITIES

Some retirees choose activities to make money. Reasons vary: some enjoy the extra income, and many younger retirees enjoying working for themselves. Others simply enjoy the process.

GIVING BACK

Many retirees find satisfaction and meaning in helping others. The opportunities are almost without limits, and the benefits range from gaining a sense of meaning and purpose to setting a good example for young people to lowering blood pressure.

GROUP/CLUB PARTICIPATION

Staying socially active is key to a healthy retirement. Reconnecting in your own community is relatively easy, but if you move to a new area, it can be difficult. Consider joining or starting a group such as a book club, investment club, or card club. Many women retirees enjoy participating in the Red Hat Society; men enjoy being in Retired Old Men Eating Out (ROMEO) groups.

One reason we strongly encourage you to start planning your retirement a few years ahead is that finding your anchoring activity can take significant lead time and require coordinating with a variety of people or organizations. For example, if you want to teach, schools are unlikely to have immediate openings, but openings may occur in the future. Also, early conversations with school administrators can help you uncover leads or opportunities to try teaching before you retire. Similarly, if a business venture is at the top of your list, you'll need time to research and organize necessary resources. Some new approaches regarding commercial ventures are tailored to retirees and are readily available on the web.

As you consider your options, remember that aside from financial risk, creating a successful business may impose other requirements, so revisit your notes regarding the things you do *not* want to do when retired.

To repeat, it takes time, good thinking, and reflection to develop a useful list. Ideally you should develop this list well before you retire. It's important to keep your list current; keeping active and satisfied for twenty to thirty years is no small trick.

As you start zeroing in on your anchor activity, think about how to manage your time. *Your time is one of your most precious assets.* As we've been saying, the rhythm of your life will change, and you'll have the time to do what you choose.

After he left a high-paced job, a friend had a revelation: "I'd just moved into what I now think of as 'stage-one' retirement—what you call 'transition'—and faced a small, simple home-maintenance problem. I finished it in about ten minutes. But as I started to walk away, I realized the fix I'd just done would probably not last for more than a month or two. I hadn't fixed it for the long term. So I stopped, went back, and spent the hour it took to really fix it, to do it right, and I felt great about it."

Another friend, an intense software entrepreneur, tells of his children teasing him with the observation that he was a "human doing," not a "human being." He got their message. His passion, or compulsion, to always be productive had gotten in the way of his being human. He says he's learning, albeit slowly, and is finding "...one key to retirement isn't that much different from the key to happiness throughout your life—to learn to live peacefully as a human being."

In the first months of your retirement, you'll likely find your personal rhythm continues similar to your work-life rhythm. This will be both from habit and circumstance, and you may have to concentrate on correcting some old habits. Your daily timetable will change—you won't be going off to your workplace. Throughout your career your activities were typically scheduled weeks, months, or even years in advance. When you step away from your life's work, you'll have to take control. If you don't, who will? In these first few months, you'll benefit greatly from paying close attention to scheduling. No longer having structured days could disconcert both you and those around you. One recent retiree offered a warning sign of a failing retirement: when you find yourself reorganizing the kitchen spice rack.

However, as time elapses, you'll find having a detailed daily schedule makes less sense, since few people will be depending on you and needing to know your schedule—other than your partner! Remember the oft-repeated and good-humored complaint: "For better or for worse but not for lunch."

Although you'll likely continue to use a daily calendar, your scheduling will involve blocks of time when you're home or away. The big decisions will be planning for changes in the activities you want to pursue. At work, your scheduling problems often entail trying to make all the things you want and need to do fit into your schedule. As you begin retirement, you'll be filling in the blocks of time among the things you've chosen to do.

You'll discover you can spend time on activities you've tended to rush for most of your life. Having time allows you to do these activities more thoughtfully. Time will be on your side, and you'll be able to delve more deeply into whatever you decide to do.

In your work life, it's likely every day has been scheduled for those with management responsibility, often down to the minute. That changes immediately. Your obligations and commitments may change gradually or suddenly. For some, the first year of retirement may offer a blank slate, promising freedom. For others, the first year may be transitional with a schedule driven by lingering commitments. Those commitments will diminish. In either case, you'll find you have blocks of free time, which lets you move activities that are satisfying and fun to the top of the list.

Finally, new technologies will be very helpful as you schedule, communicate, coordinate, and set up meetings. Although you'll have time to further develop your technology skills, a few tutorial hours with someone from the IT staff at work will surely be a more useful retirement present than a gold watch. You'll want to confirm that your passwords are secure (and where you can find them) and that your devices—phones, laptops, tablets, etc.—and their software are up to date and in good order. Similarly, it's wise to seek their advice on additional helpful applications, security measures, and their recommendation for ongoing support and advice.

We've emphasized that retirement involves a change in the very rhythm of your life and presents an unparalleled opportunity to shape a new way of life with more spontaneity and enjoyment. It may take some time to reduce your speed and find a new and comfortable rhythm. Remember, you may be living well into your eighties, and your time and your relationships are your most precious assets. And don't forget to have fun!

V

WHERE DO YOU WANT TO LIVE?

"Live where you fit."

Too often, people postpone giving any thought to where they'd like to live when retirement opens the choices. This decision warrants serious attention, the earlier the better.

Not needing to live close to work represents a new measure of freedom for some, while others find the idea of moving stressful. The prospect of relocating can be emotionally charged. You and your partner may have different ideas about your choices as well as the advantages and disadvantages of each. Your friends and acquaintances may also be considering moving. You'll need to reexamine your sense of your community, assess relationships with friends and acquaintances, and sort through the many connections you have after living years in a particular place. The National Aging in Place Council publishes a very helpful guide for sorting through these issues. (V-1)

Questions you may face include whether to move to a new location, acquire a second home, or downsize. Financial resources together with family ties and commitments will influence your thinking. For example, if you or your partner's parents are alive, you may want to stay close to them. Similarly, you may wish to stay close or relocate to be near your children and grand-children. However, be careful. Young families can be a moving target as they often relocate. Moving closer to your family can separate you from your friends. It's not uncommon for retirees to move away from where they've lived most of their lives to be with children and grandchildren and then move back.

You may anticipate health issues that will shape your decisions. If so, you should thoroughly research available healthcare facil-ities with particular attention to your specific health concerns. Similarly, changes in health may necessitate a transition to a location offering assisted living and/or long-term care. Early attention will offer peace of mind and, because many of the most desirable facilities have waiting lists, can facilitate access if the need arises.

If you live somewhere with cold winters, a warm, sunny climate may become more appealing as you age. Beyond simple com-fort, there are practical reasons why so many retirees move to or spend the winter in warmer locations. Exercising outside is easier and kinder to arthritic joints, and escaping the hazards of ice and snow lowers the chances of suffering debilitating injuries.

Upcoming retirement may bring the question of your housing needs into sharp focus. The demands of maintaining a home suitable for a larger family merit discussion with your part-ner. It's helpful to think of downsizing as having two elements: 1) your housing and 2) its contents. Although clearly linked, the considerations are largely separate. As the National Aging in Place guide emphasizes, you should decide if you want to move into a house that allows you to live on one floor. That decision is better made sooner than later under the pressure of an immediate need. Given life expectancies today, you may spend some years in a retirement community or similar facility. Many friends who resisted moving into a smaller, single-level home found they had to move into a retirement community earlier than they would've liked. If you anticipate that may be an attractive or necessary option within the next ten years, make sure your fact-finding identifies not only which appeals to you but how to get on its waiting list.

If moving to a new community seems appealing, we encourage you to give it a serious tryout before making a decision. The same advice applies to a move back to someplace once familiar but where you haven't lived for many years. Renting—ideally for a year—offers the most realistic experience against which to test your expectations. Day-to-day living in a community will help you understand if it's the right place for you. Two examples from our own experience help make the point.

> For more than thirty years, Bruce and his wife have lived in a college town in a beautiful rural area. The setting and circumstances seem idyllic, yet some who moved there when they retired found the place a bad fit. One couple discovered their love of golf was at odds with the length of winter. Another moved from New York City only to find that for them the rural charm rapidly faded with the lack of urban conveniences and the amount of driving required. Another couple discovered their social, cultural, and political views were at odds with the community's.

Ted and his wife have been friends with a couple for years. Fifteen years ago, the husband discovered he had cancer. After his successful treatment, the couple moved to Florida. The husband had several major volunteer jobs. However, when he was nearing eighty, he found few attractive opportunities. Also, he had been playing golf five days a week but found his golf game was deteriorating, which made playing less fun. He and his wife moved back up north to their hometown, resettling with old friends.

When assessing a new community, remember that retirement brings with it a different sense of your role and importance. If you've been a high achiever or in a prominent position, you're probably accustomed, perhaps unconsciously, to a certain deference and to the recognition and privileges that attend your position. Leaving your position (whether you move or not) will change that. Moving into a different community will exacerbate this shifting sense of identity. Some welcome the freedom to redefine themselves, and others find it unsettling.

If, or more likely when, you decide to downsize, be prepared for a potentially disruptive and upsetting process. You may very well be shocked at the amount of "stuff" you've accumulated. Decluttering will not be easy. Partners will likely discover quite different emotional attachments to certain possessions. You'll likely discover that your kids really *don't* want most of the stuff you thought they'd want, including items you value. The process will also take longer than you anticipate. When you complete the move to the smaller space, you'll discover you didn't dispose of nearly enough. There are dozens of "how to downsize" books; one book and a website will probably get you headed in the right direction. (V-II)

* * *

In these last three chapters, we've asked you to think through the overarching questions for planning your retirement:

- When should you retire?
- What do you want to do with your most precious asset, your time?
- Where do you want to live?

Your answers provide a framework for working through the rest of your plan. The decisions and the plans you make will be key to your finding interesting and rewarding experiences that can bring fun and fulfillment. You've likely enjoyed a challenging and rewarding life. By now we hope it's clear that planning your next chapter requires more than coming up with leisure activities. It means developing a plan adaptable enough to give you an interesting life when you enter retirement and durable enough to guide you into your eighties and nineties.

The next set of questions focuses on four dimensions: your body, your mind, your heart, and your soul. First, we'll ask you to think through how you'll maintain and preserve your physical health and fitness. Next, we'll ask you to do the same for your intellectual powers. Then we'll move to the "softer" challenges— how to preserve your emotional health and your relationships with others and, finally, that immaterial part of you, your soul, and possible paths to inner peace.

VI

MAINTAINING YOUR BODY

"If you don't take care of yourself, you can't take care of anything or anyone else."

—DR. RON GRANT

Here's the story in Bruce's words:

> Those exact words, *"If you don't take care of yourself, you can't take care of anything or anyone else,"* finally got me to pay attention to my physical condition. I was in my late forties with a wonderful wife, two great kids in good schools, a lovely home, and a big job. I'd always enjoyed good health and paid little attention to either regular exercise or to my eating and drinking habits. I was physically active, played a few sports, and kept a very busy schedule at a fast pace. I pretty much did whatever I wanted. And I used all the "I'm too busy" rationalizations for avoiding any kind of an exercise program or diet. Only when someone whom I was paying handsomely for his advice said those words to me did I really get it.

The simple truth: good health is a prerequisite for your happiness and a keystone for the rest of your life. Thus, it's where to start. That simple message convinced me to *actively* take care of myself.

First, let's consider your physical health; mental will follow. Start by asking yourself, *"Am I satisfied with my physical health?"* You must be honest in your appraisal. In this instance, a full-length mirror may help. Consider your age, your family history, your stress level, the sources of that stress, and chronic health issues. Likely you have a few minor concerns; make note of them.

AGE

....

....

FAMILY HISTORY

....

....

....

....

....

....

STRESS LEVEL

....

....

....

STRESS SOURCES

....

....

....

CHRONIC ISSUES

....

....

....

OTHER

....

....

Even if you have no significant health concerns, establishing a baseline is an essential first step. This doesn't necessarily mean three days at the Mayo Clinic. Instead, make an appointment with your primary care physician to get the process underway. In that meeting you can use the worksheet to present your sense of your health. Your physician will determine if additional information is needed to make that baseline as useful as possible. He or she may well suggest some additional tests or highlight specific issues to monitor. With that baseline, you and your physician can define your maintenance program. Your physician can identify regular needs—medications, vitamins—and establish a check-up schedule. We also recommend subscribing to one of Harvard Medical School's excellent monthly newsletters. (VI-1)

Next, consider exercise. In retirement, you'll have more time for physical activities. With your work schedule, sticking to a regular exercise routine might be difficult. Now you'll have more time and even greater motivation.

Ted recalls how he played competitive sports for most of his life but had no interest in non-sports-related exercise until he was in his forties and his work situation changed significantly. His schedule no longer accommodated group activities. He was commuting daily to Washington, DC, from Wilmington, Delaware, and found himself in a very exciting, but stressful, job. Fortunately, he discovered that regular exercise helped him sleep better and gave him a sunnier disposition. He set up a mini-gym in his basement—a stationary bike with a TV/DVD player. Later, when he retired, he worked with a personal trainer and added a Nautilus universal gym, an elliptical machine, and a treadmill. Most important, he committed to using that equipment for an hour to an hour and half at least five days a week. Retirement gave him the time and rhythm to stick to that schedule. It improved his quality of life and also gave him time to get back to playing golf, tennis, hiking, biking, walking, and water sports.

Not only will regular exercise likely help lengthen your life, it will *quickly* make you feel better and improve your life's overall quality. Your next step should be a conversation with a personal trainer. If you already know one, make an appointment. If you don't, find one. Spending money on a certified personal trainer is a wise investment. The gold standards for certification include the American Council on Exercise, the National Academy of Sports Medicine, and the National Strength and Conditioning Association. Your physician may recommend someone. You can find further sources in VI-2.

Before you meet with a trainer, summarize your physical activities. This is for your own benefit; no one is keeping score. *Don't be tempted to exaggerate.* Include sports, daily walking/running, and (if you have one) your regular exercise routine. Make notes on how often you participate in these activities and what level of exertion is involved in each. Absolute honesty with yourself will make a big difference in how much you get out of this.

Give some thought to how much time you'd like to spend on sports or other forms of exercise. Organized sports, if you enjoy them, can be a very pleasant part of your retirement. They provide essential exercise and provide social contacts. Golf, tennis, hiking, running, biking, swimming, sailing, kayaking, and other sports help you maintain your physical well-being. As you put together your plan, remember it's wise to avoid committing too much time to any one sport. What's fun to play once or twice a week could become less fun if you do it daily.

Your conversation with a trainer should be candid. Remember, this is exclusively for your benefit, not to impress anyone else. You'll describe your interests, your exercise history, and your sense of your physical condition. The trainer's goal is to build a program tailored to your needs. It will likely include aerobic exercises to maintain your cardiovascular system, weight training to slow muscle loss, and exercises to maintain balance. Since we all feel better some days more than others, be sure to ask your trainer to set up routines for "heavy" and "light" days. As you age, the types, level, and intensity of exercise will change, but this starting point greatly facilitates later adjustments.

As you organize your plan to care for your body, never forget that the odds are in favor of your living a long time. That means that almost certainly you'll experience physical problems along the way. Even a relatively minor physical problem can interfere with some sports, so it's wise to also have alternative activities. If, or, more realistically, *when,* that first reality intrusion occurs, you'll appreciate having a Plan B. The injury doesn't have to be a big deal like a blown-out ACL or a bad bike crash—all it takes is a twisted knee, bruised hip, pulled shoulder, or damaged wrist to upset your routine. You will heal, and, even though replacing joints and parts seems almost routine today, recovery takes time. As you age, recovery takes longer, and the repairs and therapy are less likely to return you to 100 percent. You may have to adjust to new circumstances, so give some thought to figuring out alternatives.

All the research tells the same story: regular exercise keeps you healthy and improves your quality of life. With your new ability to control your schedule, you can set a fitness schedule and stick to it. A couple of hints:

- Find an exercise environment you enjoy. You can exercise

outside by yourself or with others, or inside while watching TV or movies. While you work out, you can listen to audiobooks, podcasts, or music.

- Pick a time for regular exercise. If you use a fitness center or club, you'll see most people exercise in the morning. Some wait until the end of the day to reinvigorate themselves. When traveling, you'll find hotel fitness facilities jammed in the morning and free later.

Your physician and physical trainer will ask you about your eating and drinking habits. Create a list of what you do—and don't—eat and drink. Advice on what to eat is its own industry—and a particularly unregulated one. The blizzard of advice can make it hard to separate fads from science, which suggests that common sense is a good starting point. You already know the fundamentals: avoid "bad" fats, lighten up on the carbs, eat fresh fruits and vegetables, and go easy on the meat. If you believe your eating habits could benefit from a professional's assessment, ask your physician to recommend a nutritionist. Alternatively, the Academy of Nutrition and Dietetics offers a website to help you locate one near you—https://www.eatright.org.

Assessing your drinking habits may be more of a challenge. Two well-regarded organizations have websites that will help you ascertain whether you want to change anything. The first is a partnership between Boston University's School of Public Health and the Partnership for Drug-Free Kids. It only takes a few minutes to get an initial sense of direction. (VI-4) The second is a UK charity that offers a similarly quick screening. (VI-5) If you conclude you need to change your habits, it's a good idea to start by getting your physician's advice. The National Institute on Alcohol Abuse and Alcoholism also recommends a practical eleven-step approach detailed on the Harvard Health website.

As you reflect on a sensible approach to food and drink, consider the Greek poet, Hesiod. He seems to have figured it out more than 2,500 years ago, in 700 BC. His sage counsel:

"Observe due measure; moderation is best in all things."

When you think about it, that's excellent advice for just about everything we do.

As to how to maintain your body into your next chapter, the bottom line is

- Exercise.
- Eat and drink in moderation.
- Develop a sensible plan, *and then stick to it!*

VII

MAINTAINING YOUR BRAIN

"Anyone who stops learning is old, whether twenty or eighty. Anyone who keeps learning stays young. The greatest thing you can do is keep your mind young."

—MARK TWAIN

In the previous chapter, we addressed the challenges of taking care of your body, the machine that keeps you upright and functioning. Next, we'll focus on how you'll care for your brain, both its intellectual and emotional components. In this chapter, we'll address caring for the intellectual side. In the following chapter, we'll turn to the equally important and likely more complicated emotional side.

In the 1980s, Howard Gardner, a Harvard psychologist, identified eight kinds of intelligence. It's now generally accepted that every individual has multiple intelligences and that some are more developed than others. (VII-1)

Here's a cursory summary of the eight dimensions of intelligence.

- **Linguistic** or "word smart"—having particular sensitivity to words' meanings, the order among words, and their sounds, rhythms, inflections, and meter.

- **Logical-mathematical** or "numbers/reasoning smart"—the ability to conceptualize the logical relations among actions or symbols (e.g., mathematicians and scientists).
- **Spatial** or "visualization smart"—the ability to conceptualize and manipulate large-scale spatial arrays (e.g., airplane pilots, sailors) or more local forms of space (e.g., architects, chess players).
- **Bodily kinesthetic** or "body smart"—the ability to use one's whole body or parts of the body (such as the hands or the mouth) to solve problems or create products (e.g., dancers).
- **Musical** or "music smart"—sensitivity to rhythm, pitch, meter, tone, melody, and timbre and the ability to sing, play musical instruments, and compose music (e.g., conductors).
- **Interpersonal** or "people smart"—the ability to interact well with others; sensitivity to others' moods, feelings, temperaments, and motivations.
- **Intrapersonal** or "self-smart"—sensitivity to one's own feelings, goals, and anxieties, along with the capacity to plan and act in light of one's traits. Intrapersonal intelligence isn't particular to specific careers. Having intrapersonal skills helps people make consequential decisions for themselves. (More about this in the next chapter.)
- **Naturalist** or "nature smart"—the ability to make consequential distinctions in the world of nature, such as between one plant and another or one cloud formation and another (e.g., taxonomists).

What are you best at?

Figuring out your mix of intelligence will help you pick activities to keep your brain fit and provide insights about how to do it. A quick self-assessment will give you a starting point as you plan how to maintain your particular mix of intelligences.

Here are some questions you'll need to answer to take care of your cognitive abilities:

- What's your personal mix of intelligence?
- How will you maintain your mix?
- Are there other types of intelligence you would like to develop?
- What activities will best promote your intellectual health?
- Should you continue some form of your career work?
- Which relationships need attention for your intellectual health?

Next, think about how, over the years, you've developed and exercised your intelligence. We expect you'll want to keep your intelligences in as good shape as you keep your body. Consider which elements you've found most useful and important during your career. As you zero in on your principle strengths, you'll also identify other types of intelligence you have and which you feel you could further develop.

LINGUISTIC   1   2   3   4

....

....

....

LOGICAL-MATHEMATICAL   1   2   3   4

....

....

....

SPATIAL   1   2   3   4

....

....

....

BODILY KINESTHETIC   1   2   3   4

....

....

....

MUSICAL 1 2 3 4

....

....

....

INTERPERSONAL 1 2 3 4

....

....

....

INTRAPERSONAL 1 2 3 4

....

....

....

NATURALIST 1 2 3 4

....

....

....

The central question is this: what do you need to include in your retirement plans to keep your brain in shape? A recent *Harvard Health Letter* listed the following steps as central to maintaining brain health:

- Stay physically active
- Get enough sleep
- Do not smoke
- Have good social connections
- Limit alcohol consumption
- Eat a balanced diet low in saturated and trans fats

Remarkable! With one exception, *every item on this list* has to do with your *physical* condition. This is entirely consistent with current research that finds complex interconnections between physical and cognitive health. That leaves little room for doubt: to take care of your brain, you need to take care of your body. (This might be a good time to go back and reread VI!)

But what about that one exception, the benefit of maintaining social connections? What does that have to do with your brain? Research reveals that people with an active social life tend to

- Live longer—even after accounting for overall health
- Have stronger immune systems (which enables them to fight off colds, the flu, and other illnesses)
- Enjoy increased feelings of well-being and decreased feelings of depression
- Perform better on tests of memory and other cognitive skills (VII-2)

The Mayo Clinic's work also confirms that good friends are good for your health. That's consistent with common sense. Friends help you celebrate good times and provide support during bad times. They stave off loneliness and give you the chance to offer companionship. Moreover, friends can encourage you to change or avoid unhealthy lifestyle habits, such as excessive drinking or lack of exercise. (VII-3) The question becomes how will you stay connected to those you value most?

A word of caution. Social media can help you stay in touch, but it's *no* substitute for human contact.

Along with staying healthy and connected, we also need mental stimulation. Professor Cary Cooper, a UK expert in organizational psychology, tracked 3,400 retirees. His work confirmed the necessity of multiple mental stimuli. Here's a starter menu of activities offering mental stimulation:

- Do the daily puzzle, sudoku, or crossword.
- Play bridge, chess, or a challenging computer game.
- Do arithmetic in your head rather than using a calculator.
- Read. Perhaps join or start a book club. Remember, however, that not all books offer the same level of stimulation. Light reading is fine for relaxation, but the goal is to stretch and exercise your mind. Your local independent bookstore will have great suggestions; just ask.
- Try something completely new—painting, pottery, birding, photography, a new language. The list is endless.
- Take a day or evening class. If a college or university is nearby, ask about auditing their classes. (A hidden benefit: you'll find that communicating with other students, particularly younger ones, offers both mental and social stimulus.)
- Volunteer. Mentoring younger people, in particular, will keep your mind sharp.

- Teach. If you're an expert in a particular subject, teaching will be a really exciting challenge.
- Write. This includes memoirs, poetry, fiction, nonfiction, even correspondence—anything that requires you to commit your thoughts to paper (or screen).

Both Bruce and Ted certainly tried some of these activities. Bruce took flying lessons—something completely new—to satisfy a lifelong desire to know how to fly a plane. He happily confirms that flying focuses your attention and exercises your brain, particularly when landing. Ted's father was an excellent painter and spent much of his retirement creating paintings for family and friends. Ted always assumed painting would be part of his retirement, but after a few art classes, he found none of his father's talents had been passed on to him.

Another good example: a retired college professor and administrator was asked by his two grown sons, "Who were you before we knew you?" This writing challenge proved a good workout for his memory and, in his words, "a productive journey into my interior." Further, he found it a provocative challenge to explain why he is the way he is. This effort led to insights into what he wanted to change now that he had the time and freedom.

Finally, there are areas that offer both intellectual and emotional exercise, a segue to our next chapter. For instance, performing music stimulates aspects of your mind often left fallow during your career. Learning or relearning an instrument can be a satisfying intellectual challenge. And then playing (or singing) with others in larger ensembles provides social connection. As well, attending performances and concerts engages both your intellectual and emotional brain. The same holds true for going to the theater or cinema with others and discussing afterward what you've seen. Multiplayer card games—bridge or poker—also can keep your brain sharp while allowing you to stay in touch with others.

Even though some research shows aging may start to affect the brain in one's forties, the odds are heavily in your favor that you'll begin your next chapter with your particular mix of intelligences in good shape. There's no question that as the years pass, aging will eventually have its way, which is why this planning is imperative. The most important lesson is that *all* current research confirms keeping your body and brain fit will help put off aging's effects.

As you move through your late sixties and into your seventies, you'll likely become aware of mental changes. Or your good friends or partner will point them out to you. While this can be initially disconcerting, you'll observe your friends sharing similar experiences—forgotten names, misplaced keys, and other "senior moments." But don't overreact! Too many people self-diagnose this natural phenomenon as the beginning of Alzheimer's or dementia. If you need it for your peace of mind, a talk with your physician can help, but keep in mind that Alzheimer's and dementia affect only 7 percent of people over sixty-five.

Finally, it's important to remain positive. Yale University Professor Becca Levy's respected study conducted over twenty years in Ohio found that those who viewed aging as a positive experience lived seven and a half years longer than those with more pessimistic attitudes. (VII-4)

Now, on to planning how you'll care for your emotional dimensions.

VIII

MAINTAINING YOUR HEART

"No road is long with good company."

—TURKISH PROVERB

We're *not* talking about your physical heart, the organ of interest to your cardiologist. We *are* talking about your emotional heart, the heart that moves you to tears seeing the birth of your child, the heart that swells with pride watching your daughter graduate, and the heart that warms you when an old friend makes a surprise visit. This heart is your emotional core—an essential but challenging area for planning your retirement.

We understand that many people dealing with the rational, logical work of keeping your body and brain fit is more comfortable than moving to the "softer" side and learning how to keep yourself emotionally fit. Entering your emotional sphere involves setting aside familiar habits of thought and comfortable layers of protection. This area for attention can pose difficult and potentially frustrating challenges for everyone, men and women alike. This is a considerably more complicated planning challenge because you are likely more complicated than you think. Try asking Google, "Why are feelings so complicated?"

The previous chapter introduced the importance of social connectedness. This chapter will focus on the social dimension—how you stay connected and maintain good relationships with the outside world, your family, friends, and others. In the next chapter, we'll move to the challenge of your interior dimension.

When you leave your career and the life that went with it, you step into a different world. As we've emphasized, the changes retirement brings are profound and involve significant emotional adjustments. Let's recap the central ideas we introduced in II.

- When you retire, you leave the relationships, satisfactions, and support systems you enjoy in your work life.

These relationships, satisfactions, and support systems bring with them emotional shifts. Relationships change or end; you no longer experience certain pleasures and positive reinforcements; and losing support systems requires you to be self-sufficient.

- Your role, position, and status changes.

The extent to which you and others link your identity to your work may surprise you. It's likely you take for granted the authority and influence that accompanies your work responsibilities. You enjoy a certain status in the workplace and in your personal life. You may have a lot of authority, and you may have expertise in your field. Possessing authority and expertise doesn't encourage humility. But humility nourishes relationships and can be of great value as you seek satisfaction and meaningfulness. (VIII-1)

- You have less structure and thus more choices.

Work shapes and structures your daily, weekly, monthly, and annual routines; your commitments; and vacations. Now the choices will be all yours, perhaps on the first day of your retirement but certainly by the end of the first year.

- You need to find a new rhythm for your life.

Imagine your career as marching at a steady pace with frequent bursts of double-time and occasional sprints. Now the music stops. The choices are yours. Keep marching? At what pace? To where?

- Your life will change, certainly situationally and perhaps geographically.

Given all these changes, your emotional equilibrium will be tested. To realize your objective—a satisfying, enjoyable, and fulfilling next chapter of your life—there is simply no escape from dealing with this change.

Here are some questions to consider regarding maintaining your relationships and your emotional health:

- Which are your key relationships now? Which will they be after retirement?
- Which relationships are the most challenging?
- Which relationships need strengthening? More attention?
- How will your relationship map (see below) change over time?
- Are there aspects of your emotional intelligence you wish to strengthen? (VIII-2)
- How do your networking talents transfer into retirement?

Two exercises can help you shape your answers. The first is a quick self-assessment of your emotional intelligence. Think of your emotional intelligence as your ability to recognize, understand, and influence your own emotions, as well as the emotions of others. Current research points to five dimensions of emotional intelligence for your self-assessment:

- **Self-awareness** is the ability to know your emotions, strengths, weaknesses, drives, values, and goals. As well, it concerns recognizing the impact of your emotional attributes on others. It also entails using your emotions to inform your decisions.
- **Self-regulation** involves controlling or redirecting your disruptive emotions and impulses and adapting to changing circumstances.
- **Social skills** entail managing relationships to move people, read social situations, and interact effectively.
- **Empathy** means perceiving others' feelings and perspectives especially when communicating and making decisions.
- **Motivation** means using your own attributes to achieve your goals and overcome adversities.

This self-assessment should help you recognize the aspects of emotional intelligence you possess. You can do a quick self-assessment here; however, the website Mind Tools offers a very helpful fifteen-item quiz. (VIII-3)

SELF-AWARENESS   1   2   3   4   5

....

....

....

SELF-REGULATION 1 2 3 4 5

....

....

....

SOCIAL SKILLS 1 2 3 4 5

....

....

....

EMPATHY 1 2 3 4 5

....

....

....

MOTIVATION 1 2 3 4 5

....

....

....

The following illustration shows the second exercise to help you identify your priorities in relationships. On a large sheet of paper, draw five concentric circles. You are in the center. In the second circle, put the names of those closest to you—likely your partner and one or two others whom you consider your most intimate friends. The third circle is for close family members and others with whom you share strong bonds. Include in the fourth circle those you think of as casual friends. The fifth circle includes your community: social acquaintances, neighbors, club members. Outside these concentric circles sits society at large, the rest of the world.

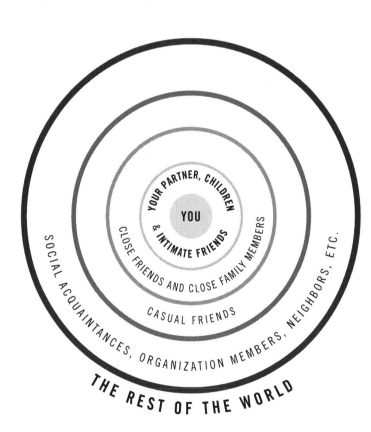

In effect, this is your relationship map, and retirement will require you to redraw it. As you look at yours, consider your relationships with others, how they'll change, and what to do. (Keep in mind that this is an important consideration as you decide where to live.) Satisfying relationships are an essential part of a fulfilling retirement, so it pays to think carefully about the people you wish to be closer to during your retirement years.

In general, your social and professional relationships will change for several reasons:

- Proximity. How often you see or talk to certain people will change.
- Change in status. Your position in your workplace, whether one of authority or not, influences how you interact with others and they with you. This will change.
- The people and systems who assist you as you deal with others will no longer be there.

Working through these questions yields a relationship to-do list. Personal relationships are complex and difficult to change. As you build your list, make notes about whether the need is urgent, important, or both. You may find you want to add another criterion—*uncomfortable*. For many, the toughest work is examining these especially personal areas. You may find your partner or a close friend could help you with this.

However, you may find it helpful to consider professional assistance. No, we're not saying you "need a shrink." Just as we recommended getting a physical trainer to help you plan how to maintain your body, we're suggesting that the skilled outside voice of a therapist can ease this task. The therapist's goal is to help you make decisions and clarify feelings in order to solve problems. For this kind of help, you will want to find a qualified therapist with whom you are comfortable. How do you find the right therapist? *Psychology Today* and NBC News have both addressed this question and offer sound advice. (VIII-4)

Consider all your relationships as you go through this process. Some will become closer, and some will become more distant. Your responsibility is to consider what you want. Perhaps you want more time with certain friends or to reconnect with someone you care about. In some cases, this requires a frank discussion with yourself about how your relationships currently function and how—and why—you want them to change.

Now it's time to turn inward. The remaining challenge is to determine what you need to make this next phase of your life meaningful.

IX

MAINTAINING YOUR SOUL

"To live happily is an inward power of the soul."

—MARCUS AURELIUS

In the preceding chapters, we've focused on how you will maintain physical, intellectual, and emotional fitness to care for your body, your mind, and your relationships. Now we turn inward and focus on the soul, the interior "you." This is *not* about following a particular religion, belief system, or philosophy. This is about one question: what will make you believe you live a meaningful life? Only you can determine what gives your life meaning—what makes your existence important, significant, and worthwhile.

Perhaps you find meaning in your familial relationships or through the difference you've made during your working life or through your good works. Psychologist Stephanie Hooker explains *meaning* this way: "…basically the idea that your life makes sense, you're here for a reason, and you're significant in the world." While some individuals manage to defer this until they're much older, recent research confirms that around age sixty, many people begin reflecting on their life's meaning. That suggests you might start paying attention to the question before you retire. (IX-1)

We encourage you to do so, and we hope to help as you read the following pages. To start, there's a growing body of hard evidence showing the physical benefits of spirituality.

Numerous scientific studies show that spirituality helps improve your health, including lower blood pressure, a healthier immune system, increased longevity, and better mental health. But what do we mean when we talk about spirituality? The University of Minnesota's Bakken Center offers this explanation:

> Spirituality is a broad concept with room for many perspectives. In general, it includes a sense of connection to something bigger than ourselves, and it typically involves a search for meaning in life. As such, it is a universal human experience—something that touches us all. People may describe a spiritual experience as sacred or transcendent or simply a deep sense of aliveness and interconnectedness. Some may find that their spiritual life is intricately linked to their association with a church, temple, mosque, or synagogue. Others may pray or find comfort in a personal relationship with God or a higher power. Still others seek meaning through their connections to nature or art. (IX-2)

Clearly, spirituality is a "big tent" accommodating many different paths to the common goal—the individual's sense of meaning. It isn't just church or religion. It can be found in nature, in art, and by serving others. The list is long, and the message is clear: *whatever you find solace or comfort in is what's right for you.*

While this may seem outside the realm of science, evidence

continues to build that people who make the effort to develop their spirituality tend to cope better with life's challenges and experience less stress in their daily lives. Having a sense of purpose allows them this.

- An Oxford University study summed it up best. "Spirituality is an integral dimension of human beings and has been recognized as a critical factor in the health and well-being of patients. Numerous studies have demonstrated a relationship between spirituality and a variety of patient outcomes including quality of life and coping with illness."
- Another study in *Cancer,* a journal of the American Cancer Society, "…suggests a link between religious or spiritual beliefs and better physical health reported among patients with cancer." The lead author notes, "In our observational study, we found people who found feelings of transcendence or meaningfulness or peace reported feeling the least physical problems."
- At the University of Missouri, researchers gathered people from different faith traditions—including Buddhists, Catholics, Jews, Muslims, and Protestants—to see if there were any differences in health outcomes. They discovered that increased spirituality was "significantly related" to better mental health, regardless of what form the spirituality took.
- In a collaborative study among professors at Columbia University and the New York State Psychiatric Institute, researchers report a direct correlation between the importance of spirituality in a person's life and the thickness of their cerebral cortex—the part of the brain responsible for sensory perception, language, and emotion processing.

Again, here's the central question for you to answer: what will it take for you to feel you've led a meaningful life? Exploring what will provide you with meaning may be the most complex, personal, and imprecise leg of this entire journey.

To stimulate your curiosity and help you get started, we've summarized a few books and websites that span belief systems and approaches. We hope this will encourage your further exploration and eventual discovery.

- *The Book of Joy* is by two Nobel Peace Prize laureates: the Dalai Lama, a Tibetan Buddhist, and Archbishop Desmond Tutu, a South African Anglican (Protestant). The book captures the extraordinary conversation between the Dalai Lama and Archbishop Desmond Tutu over two days celebrating the Dalai Lama's eightieth birthday. Their subject was how to find joy in a world filled with adversity. The book is a very readable and enjoyable combination of insights, examples, and extraordinarily funny exchanges. You certainly do not have to be a Buddhist or an Episcopalian to profit from their insights as you develop your retirement plan. (IX-3)
- The second book, *Creating a Spiritual Retirement* by Molly Strode, offers helpful insights in retirement. The guiding principle is that in many countries and religions, the last third of life is dedicated to a search for the path to finding one's soul and thus makes this phase of our lives more meaningful. The book concentrates on helping gain a deeper understanding of how we should live our lives. Chapters focus on "The Individual Spirit," "The Great Spirit," and "Practical Spirituality" with practical ways to search for spiritual peace that provide support in this important time in our lives. *Creating a Spiritual Retirement* has a website that can be used as a guide. (IX-4)
- *Aging as a Spiritual Practice* by Lewis Richmond centers

on Buddhist thoughts, but believing in Buddhism is by no means a prerequisite! Richmond discusses aging, acknowledging the fear, anger, and sorrow many people experience when they must confront the indignities of their aging bodies and mortality. He suggests four key stages of aging:

- **Lightning Strikes**: The moment we truly wake up to our aging.
- **Coming to Terms**: Comparing ourselves now to how we once were.
- **Adaptation**: Letting go of who we were and embracing who we are.
- **Appreciation**: Acknowledging that "This is my life, I have no other."

Whether you're enjoying growing old, hating it, or in denial, each chapter has relatable anecdotes, including Richmond's own experiences. His guided meditations and thoughts about how we can't escape life's essential problems can change our understanding about them and help us enjoy the process. (IX-5)

- *Man's Search for Meaning* by Viktor Frankl, an Auschwitz survivor who wrote this small book in 1946. This book is by no means an easy read but is important and powerful. Frankl says the core responsibility of our individual human lives is to find meaning and purpose, not just in fame or wealth but in transcendent ways, through faith, hope, and, most importantly, love. (IX-6)
- *Why Buddhism Is True* by Robert Wright conveys the benefits of meditation. *The New York Times Book Review* described it this way:

Written with wit, clarity, and grace and as entertaining

as it is illuminating. Wright shows how meditation can loosen the grip of anxiety, regret, and hatred, and how it can deepen your appreciation of beauty and of other people. [Wright]…lays the foundation for a spiritual life in a secular age and shows how, in a time of technological distraction and social division, we can save ourselves from ourselves, both as individuals and as a species. He also shows why this transformation works, drawing on the latest in neuroscience and psychology, and armed with an acute understanding of human evolution. (IX-7)

* * *

Several websites can help you further explore spirituality and the pursuit of a meaningful life:

- Well Beyond 55 echoes a message earlier in this chapter:
  - "Spirituality is a very broad tent. To some, it means attending religious services regularly and practicing the traditions of an established religion. To others, it could mean simply being still and allowing the universe to speak to them in that silence—often referred to as meditation. However you define spirituality, it appears to have a positive effect on one's health."
  - The website says meditation helps people attain spirituality, citing studies that found meditation created physical changes in the brain. It cites a UCLA study showing that a three-month course of yoga and meditation helped minimize the cognitive issues that often precede Alzheimer's disease and other forms of dementia.
- The Esquiline, although a website for practicing Catholics, offers wise, practical tips for everyone. For example,

- "As you age, the shape of your life naturally changes. So does your relationship to religion and spirituality.
- Keep asking questions. Why do you believe what you believe? What would help strengthen your faith? What could you do differently?
- Give thanks. Don't forget to take a moment every day to reflect on what you're grateful for.
- Take time to reflect. Not only is it a fulfilling exercise, but it's beneficial to your mental and physical health.
- Stay optimistic. Your faith or spirituality can help comfort you in difficult times and inspire you during good times.
- If you believe in a higher power, pray. It's a simple act of faith, but sometimes we forget how much it can affect our spirituality." (IX-8)
- Ken Jones's website Ageing: the Great Adventure—A Buddhist Guide, like the above, offers helpful insights for everyone, whatever their belief system. In particular, he discusses the negative portrayal of aging throughout our popular culture but rejects it, arguing
  - "Aging can be the culminating adventure of our lives, up to which the earlier years may be seen as a preparation. I do not refer here to the promise of perpetual youth peddled by golden oldie consumerism. That is more evasion than adventure. The adventure of aging is nothing less than the opportunity to transcend the self which has lived its life up to now, and hence to transcend the decrepitude and death of that self. At its simplest that grand word 'transcendence' is about being totally at ease with ourselves, and hence at ease with others. Freed from self-preoccupations and anxieties we can wholeheartedly serve others."
  - The website includes training, skills, and practices to make an "art of growing old." (IX-9)

* * *

In sum, there is so much evidence from such diverse and respected sources that your question should not be whether to address spirituality but only how best to do it for you. Your objective is both a *satisfying* and a *meaningful* retirement. We hope we've shown here how they are interconnected and, we believe, indivisible.

X

PULLING IT TOGETHER

"You only live once, but if you do it right, once is enough."

—MAE WEST

This guidebook offers you a way to gather important information about yourself. Your challenge is to shape this information into a useful and durable form. Rest easy. There's no single right way to do this. Whatever you come up with now is subject to change as reality unfolds. The only test that matters is what will work best for you. As we've repeatedly emphasized, every retirement is unique, and how you plan yours is up to you.

Very different approaches can accomplish a successful result. To make that point, we'll explain how we, two very different individuals, did it. Ted, a 1960 Duke graduate, and Bruce, a 1961 Brown graduate, were classmates at Wharton, where they received their MBAs in 1966. They then traveled very different paths. Similarly, when it came to planning and shaping their retirements, their approaches reflected those differences. Ted, an engineer by training, took an analytical and methodical approach, while Bruce's approach was more free-form and creative. As you read the two stories, you'll see how in very different ways we each worked through the questions and issues we've built into this guide to yield successful, satisfying, fun, and meaningful retirements.

TED'S STORY

First, some background. After Wharton, I returned to DuPont and spent seven years in marketing, engineering, and finance positions. My involvement in Delaware politics led to a dramatic career change in 1973 when twenty-nine-year-old Joe Biden won the US Senate seat. He asked me to join him to help build his staff, which led to spending the next twenty-two years commuting with him to Washington, DC, with nineteen of those years as his Chief of Staff.

Now my retirement story. In 1987, Senator Biden was chair of the Judiciary Committee, and we'd hired a Duke Law constitutional scholar, Chris Schroeder, to help us prepare for the Bork Supreme Court nomination hearings. Chris and I worked well together, and in 1990, he asked if I'd teach a course on the Congress with him at Duke Law School. I said I'd love to but being Chief of Staff to a major senator was much more than a full-time job, so I had to pass. He told me to take a few days to think about it.

I talked to my wife, Lynne, and she agreed it would be difficult. But this discussion segued into an ongoing discussion about how long I'd continue to work in the Senate. I loved my job and working for Senator Biden, but we agreed it was time for me to figure out what I'd do with the rest of my life. That agreement led to concluding that if I was going to retire in five or six years, teaching at Duke would be a wonderful beginning to my/our retirement. I told Senator Biden the class would require lots of preparation, but I'd only be away from the DC office for nine Mondays when I'd commute to Duke to teach. He thought it was a great idea. Duke's Sanford School of Public Policy signed on as partners for the class, and in early 1991, Chris and I started teaching our course, The Congress, to a class of law and public policy students. Teaching proved to be the anchor activity of my retirement. In various capacities, I ended up teaching at Duke for twenty-six years.

During that first year at Duke, I started looking ahead and knew I would not be ready for anything like a traditional retirement for a long time. I just wanted complete control over my schedule. To that end, in 1991 I started building what I called my 1995 Venture Plan, a list of potential activities. I updated it regularly as ideas came from all kinds of sources—mostly business associates and friends—and I spent considerable time thinking about what I might do. Many ideas didn't survive a closer look—joining a DC lobby firm, chartering a boat to go down the Intercoastal Waterway, joining a string band—but a good number proved right for me and my family. In 1995, I left Biden's Senate office and began teaching a second course at Duke's Fuqua School of Business. The next twelve years included

- Starting Duke Law School's Center for the Study of Congress.
- Serving on the US Broadcasting Board of Governors.
- Helping plan Senator Biden's reelection campaign.
- Partnering in online resources computer search firm.
- Serving on several for-profit and nonprofit boards.
- Organizing a hiking, biking, and kayaking group.
- Writing a weekly column in the local paper.

And, very importantly, I spent a lot more time with my family and enjoyed a greatly expanded vacation schedule.

My retirement was interrupted when Delaware governor Minner appointed me to fill Biden's seat in the US Senate when he became vice president. From 2008 through 2010, I served on the Foreign Relations, Armed Services, Judiciary, and Budget committees.

Lynne and I decided to stay in Wilmington because we didn't want to move away from our longtime friends. Our plan was to spend two winter months in Florida and two summer weeks on the New Jersey shore. We downsized, moving into a house in which we could live on one floor but with upstairs space for visiting family and friends. The new house had a spacious basement that we used for our new collection of physical training equipment.

Golf, tennis, hiking, and walking provide us with physical and social benefits. We visit children and grandchildren in the US and UK and spend two months during the winter in Vero Beach, Florida, and two summer weeks with family in Stone Harbor, New Jersey. We take one or two trips a year with family or friends. We've reserved an apartment in a retirement community starting in 2023.

And now that I'm eighty-one, the Venture Plan is up to date and my retirement includes

- Leading the Biden transition planning; assisting the Biden presidential campaign; chairing the Biden Foundation.
- Writing a column for the Wilmington *News Journal*.
- Serving on the Institute for International Education board, the Scholar Rescue Fund board, and the Ministry of Caring board.
- Volunteering at Catholic charities.

I start most days attending Mass and end most days with an hour or more workout. I play golf weekly in season, lunch regularly with old friends, and meditate regularly. Life is good.

BRUCE'S STORY

Unlike my good friend (and engineer), Ted, I don't recall ever putting anything on paper that would qualify as a plan. Key to my story: for fifty-seven years I've been blessed with a remarkable partner. Ginny shared navigating my unusual career, shared successfully parenting our two children, and shared creating our next chapter. As well, Ginny earned an MPH at Yale School of Public Health, did "corporate wife" duty, and served nonprofit organizations every place we lived.

First, a quick career profile: my McKinsey & Co. experience shaped my career as an independent consultant. I enjoyed long-term relationships working alongside CEOs helping improve their top management team performance and updating corporate strategies and practices. Major clients included the New York Stock Exchange, Time Inc., JC Penney, and FMC. In the mid-eighties I took a break from consulting and spent five years as Chief Administrative Officer of Time Inc. In 1987, I returned to consulting, working with the New York Stock Exchange's chairman to strengthen his management team and plan his succession.

Now my retirement tale. My first attempt at retiring came from the confluence of two events. In 1987, along with my return to consulting, we'd bought a "fun farm" in Cornwall, Vermont, a town adjoining Middlebury, home of Middlebury College. Our original plan was to have a place to escape the New York City (NYC) sphere of influence, but our first family gathering in Vermont at Thanksgiving led all four of us to conclude we'd rather live in a beautiful Vermont college town than Manhattan. Since I could easily fly to/from NYC, we moved to Vermont five months later. Since my client planned to retire in two years, I could see a natural conclusion to that assignment and commuting weekly from Vermont to NYC. I concluded I was ready to retire from management consulting. I was in my early fifties, fit, and longing for a new kind of labor that, in contrast to consulting, would produce tangible (and sometimes edible) results.

In 1989, that first retirement started on schedule—and lasted for only six months when the new NYSE chairman summoned me back. I realized that in those six months I'd satisfied my need to do physical labor. I also realized I actually needed intellectually challenging work. In retrospect, that "mini-sabbatical" allowed us to sort out what to do in my/our next chapter. I limited my NYC consulting to half-time and started to research my options. Actually, "research" is much too formal a term for what amounted to poking around.

As luck would have it, in the 1970s, a business investment I'd made (to help write off ski vacations) provided me a sense of Vermont's opportunities, needs, and cultural landscape. All resonated with my/our values and interests. Vermont is a very small state, and the local wisdom is that everyone knows everyone else or knows someone who does. It didn't take long for me to be sized up and get connected. Then opportunities surfaced.

Community involvement seems part of my DNA and had always been an important extra-curricular for me. Out of curiosity, I attended a local school board meeting and asked a few questions. Next I knew, I was drafted by concerned locals to take over the board and oust an ineffectual school principal. The job leading the local school board put me on the regional school district executive committee, an ideal way to learn about local politics. A blessedly unsuccessful run for the Vermont legislature showed me I lacked the patience, style, and temperament for that version of politics.

I easily found mental stimulation and socialization. Members of the Middlebury College faculty and administration were welcoming while, on the business side, I was an angel investor in four startups. Each offered its own challenges, and all were satisfying even though not necessarily profitable. The most fulfilling was helping ten dairy farm families build a premium milk business. They taught me the challenges of dairy farming and, in turn, they learned the business challenge of food marketing and distribution. Early on I was invited into a partnership that owned Middlebury's historic anchor building. When the managing partner moved west, I had to learn the real estate business. That led to reorganizing and chairing the local business association and building a partnership with Middlebury College's president, who shared our concerns about the local economy.

My second retirement began in 2002 as I ended my long entanglement with New York and the corporate world. My consulting work had shifted to helping the NYSE's subsidiary, SIAC (Securities Industry Automation Corporation) cope with the impact of technology, an important but not personally satisfying task. Concurrently, my ninety-year-old parents moved to Vermont for their final years. After the 9/11 event, I stepped away from my career's work to help care for my parents and continue with Vermont business and community responsibilities.

During this retirement, Ginny and I traveled extensively and enjoyed our extended family. My skills continued to prove useful at the local level. I'd become head of our town government only to discover a gas pipeline company intent on bisecting our town's historic center. Our community team stopped them. In 2014, we started adjusting to age by renovating a smaller house closer to town and downsizing.

The most recent retirement started in early 2017 at age seventy-eight. I sold the downtown historic building and stepped back from all community boards, offices, and involvements. We now divide our time between Vermont and Vero Beach, Florida. Together, we share the challenge of dealing with aging and the joys of harvesting the fruits of our labors. My relationship with my wife, our two children, their spouses, and our four grandchildren—together with the intangible rewards of community service—continue to satisfy my need for a sense of meaning. My soul reports that it is happy, comfortable, and content.

∗ ∗ ∗

As those two stories reveal, we took two very different approaches, but along the way we addressed the same questions. Now it's your turn. As you begin, remember that when it comes to shaping the next chapter of your life, there are *no* universal, generic, all-purpose, surefire methods. Nor answers. Nor formats. You may prefer getting it down on paper to help compare alternatives or sort out conflicts. Or you may find that, as one friend put it, "my plan kind of happened." The right way is whatever works for you in your circumstances.

XI

LOOKING FURTHER AHEAD

"Old age: the crown of life, our play's last act."
—MARCUS TULLIUS CICERO

Your main focus should be on this book's first ten chapters. It makes sense now to concentrate your energy and efforts on planning how you will achieve a satisfying and fulfilling retirement.

Later in retirement—where we are—you'll face new challenges that will require similar planning. The changes will most probably start to occur when you're in your seventies, although the precise age varies greatly among individuals. What you will want to have in place are contingency plans and options so you can maintain an active and rewarding life.

The rhythm of your life will change again, and you may find you seek more time walking, reading, and enjoying time with family and friends. You may discover you're gradually adopting a life of contemplation and humility. Many of our friends say these can be the best years of your life. A friend shared the story of her grandfather who lived actively, walking in Rittenhouse

Park every day and immersed in charity work until his last six weeks. He had three rules:

- Surround yourself with people of all ages.
- Have interests beyond your family because family members have their own lives to lead.
- Learn something new every day.

At some point you'll probably begin to experience some physical and mental limitations. For instance, you may begin to find travel more difficult and instead wish to seek activities that reduce stress. You may no longer want to take on complex responsibilities that require you to lead and redefine your involvement so that you're active but not in charge. You may look for opportunities to use what you've learned to help others.

Bruce found the most fulfilling work he'd ever done began when he was seventy-seven. Through the Winners Walk Tall program, he works with underprivileged fifth graders, teaching them basic social skills—a firm handshake and eye contact—and social values such as hard work and not cheating. He's found the results for both himself and the kids remarkable.

Ted has found one of the best things he's done at this age is to bookend his days. Just about every day he gets up to have breakfast and attend Mass at our local church. And he ends practically every day with over an hour working out in his gym.

Later—usually around your mid-eighties—you'll find you have less energy and likely other limitations that require you to cut back on travel and other activities. You may have stopped driving, or you may need assistance in your home, or you need to move to a retirement community. Your independence will likely be compromised. Your planning for these years should include finding a place that can provide daily medical care if needed. The best places tend to have long waiting lists but allow you to join the wait list for a small deposit. Many of our friends have had to move somewhere that wasn't their top choice because they didn't plan ahead.

Keep in mind the transitions between these stages. The most important thing to remember is *when* you move from one life stage to another may well be beyond your control, especially if changes occur suddenly. Just as in your earlier life, you need a plan for these transitions.

Consideration of one's soul and spirituality almost inevitably leads to reflection about the end of life, the last chapter. British philosopher Bertrand Russell wrote this at age eighty-one and went on to live another sixteen years. Herewith is his counsel on how to grow old and deal with death:

> The best way to overcome [the fear of death]—so at least it seems to me—is to make your interests gradually wider and more impersonal, until bit by bit the walls of the ego recede, and your life becomes increasingly merged in the universal life.

> An individual human existence should be like a river: small at first, narrowly contained within its banks, and rushing passionately past rocks and over waterfalls. Gradually the river grows wider, the banks recede, the waters flow more quietly, and in the end, without any visible break, they become merged in the sea, and painlessly lose their individual being.

> The person who, in old age, can see life in this way, will not suffer from the fear of death, since the things he or she cares for will

continue. And if, with the decay of vitality, weariness increases, the thought of rest will not be unwelcome.

I should wish to die while still at work, knowing that others will carry on what I can no longer do and content in the thought that what was possible has been done. (XI-1)

* * *

The new retirement will bring many changes. The one constant is that those who enjoy a satisfying and meaningful retirement are those who applied their thinking and planning talents to the challenge.

Appendix A

CHAPTER RESOURCES

II

1. Dina Gerdeman, "Welcome to Retirement. Who Am I Now?" Business Research for Business Leaders, Harvard Business School, September 17, 2018, https://hbswk.hbs.edu/item/welcome-to-retirement-who-am-i-now?utm_source=SilverpopMailing&utm_medium=email&utm_campaign=Daily Gazette 20180918; Grant Freeland, "How To Avoid 'Former Leader Syndrome': Start While You're Still A Leader," https://www.forbes.com/sites/grantfreeland/2019/04/01/how-to-avoid-former-leader-syndrome-start-while-youre-still-a-leader/#5db88d2b61aa; Carol Hymowitz, "Looking for a Road Map to Retirement? Good Luck with That," *Wall Street Journal*, https://www.wsj.com/articles/looking-for-a-road-map-for-retirement-good-luck-with-that-11560737160.

2. Karen Wagner and Erica Baird, "What Surprises Boomer Women Professionals When They Retire," *Forbes,* published July 2, 2018, https://www.forbes.com/sites/nextavenue/2018/07/02/what-surprises-boomer-women-professionals-when-they-retire/#7e0ad6ba19dc; Larry Swedroe and Katie

Keary, "The Unique Retirement Issues Facing Women," Advisor Perspectives, published July 30, 2018, https://www.advisorperspectives.com/articles/2018/07/30/the-unique-retirement-issues-facing-women; Karen Wagner and Erica Baird, "Adjusting to Retirement: 4 Ways Women Professionals Can Get Over the Hump," Next Avenue, published July 9, 2018, https://www.nextavenue.org/adjusting-retirement-women-professionals/.

III

1. Neil Schneiderman, Gail Ironson, Scott D. Siegel, "Stress and Health: Psychological, Behavioral, and Biological Determinants," *Annual Review of Clinical Psychology* 1 (2005): 607–28, DOI: 10.1146/annurev.clinpsy.1.102803.144141.

2. "Stress Assessments," NYSUT Social Services, accessed October 17, 2020, https://www.nysut.org/~/media/files/nysut/resources/2013/april/social-services/socialservices_stressassessments.pdf?la=en.

3. Arthur C. Brooks, "Your Professional Decline Is Coming (Much) Sooner Than You Think," *The Atlantic,* published July 2019, https://www.theatlantic.com/magazine/archive/2019/07/work-peak-professional-decline/590650/.

4. Roberta K. Taylor and Dorian Mintzer, *The Couples Retirement Puzzle: 10 Must-Have Conversations for Transitioning to the Second Half of Life* (Waltham, MA: Lincoln Street Press, 2011).

5. Roberta K. Taylor and Dorian Mintzer, *The Couples Retirement Puzzle: 10 Must-Have Conversations for Transitioning to the Second Half of Life* (Waltham, MA: Lincoln Street Press, 2011).

IV

1. Mark Evan Chimsky, *65 Things to Do When You Retire* (Portland, ME: Sellers Publishing, 2012).

V

1. "Act III: Your Plan for Aging in Place," National Aging in Place Council, accessed October 17, 2020, https://www.ageinplace.org/Portals/0/pdf/aging_in_place_planning_guide_final_8-14-1.pdf.
2. "Downsizing the Family Home: What to Save, What to Let Go," My Move, updated July 30, 2020, https://www.mymove.com/moving/guides/senior-guide-downsizing/.

VI

1. "Harvard Men's Health Watch," Harvard Health Publishing, Harvard Medical School, accessed October 17, 2020, https://www.health.harvard.edu/newsletters/harvard_mens_health_watch.
2. Jamie King, "10 Things to Consider Before Choosing a Personal Trainer," *The Huffington Post,* updated January 6, 2015, https://www.huffpost.com/entry/choosing-a-personal-trainer_b_6085318; "How to Choose the Right Personal Trainer," American Council on Exercise, published January 28, 2009, https://www.acefitness.org/education-and-resources/lifestyle/blog/6624/how-to-choose-the-right-personal-trainer.
3. "Thinking about Drinking? Curious about What's Healthy?" Alcohol Screening, Center on Addiction, accessed October 17, 2020, https://alcoholscreening.org.
4. "Are You Drinking Too Much?" Drinkaware, accessed October 17, 2020, https://www.drinkaware.co.uk.

VII

1. "The Official Authoritative Site of Multiple Intelligences," MI Oasis, accessed October 17, 2020, https://www.multipleintelligencesoasis.org.

2. Yang Claire Yang, et al., "Social Relationships and Physiological Determinants of Longevity across the Human Life Span," *Proceedings of the National Academy of Sciences of the United States of America* 113, no. 3 (2016): 578–83, DOI: 10.1073/pnas.1511085112.

3. Mayo Clinic Staff, "Friendships: Enrich Your Life and Improve Your Health," Mayo Clinic, accessed October 17, 2020, https://www.mayoclinic.org/healthy-lifestyle/adult-health/in-depth/friendships/art-20044860.

4. Awais Aftab, et al., "Meaning in Life and Its Relationship with Physical, Mental, and Cognitive Functioning: A Study of 1,042 Community-Dwelling Adults Across the Lifespan," *The Journal of Clinical Psychiatry* 81, no. 1 (2020), https://doi.org/10.4088/JCP.19m13064.

VIII

1. Dina Gerdeman, "Welcome to Retirement. Who am I Now?" Harvard Business School, published September 17, 2018, https://hbswk.hbs.edu/item/welcome-to-retirement-who-am-i-now?utm_source=SilverpopMailing&utm_medium=email&utm_campaign=Daily Gazette 20180918.

2. Harvard Professional Development, "Assessing Your Emotional Intelligence: 4 Tools We Love," Harvard Division of Continuing Education, published November 18, 2016, https://www.extension.harvard.edu/professional-development/blog/assessing-your-emotional-intelligence-4-tools-we-love.

3. "How Emotionally Intelligent Are You? Boosting Your People

Skills," Mind Tools, accessed October 17, 2020, https://www.mindtools.com/pages/article/ei-quiz.htm.

4. Tracey Cleantis, "How to Find the Best Therapist for You: Seven Tips on Finding the Best Fit for You," *Psychology Today*, published February 16, 2011, https://www.psychologytoday.com/us/blog/freudian-sip/201102/how-find-the-best-therapist-you; Nicole Spector, "How to Find the Right Therapist: What's Perhaps the Most Important Qualification in Finding the Right Therapist? Your Own Intuition," Better by Today, published August 5, 2018, https://www.nbcnews.com/better/health/how-find-right-therapist-ncna896111.

IX

1. University of Minnesota Bakken Center, https://www.csh.umn.edu/.

2. "What Is Spirituality?" Taking Charge of Your Health and Well-Being, University of Minnesota, accessed October 17, 2020, https://www.takingcharge.csh.umn.edu/what-spirituality.

3. Dalai Lama, Desmond Tutu, and Douglas Carlton Abrams, *The Book of Joy: Lasting Happiness in a Changing World* (New York: Avery, 2016).

4. Molly Strode, *Creating a Spiritual Retirement: A Guide to the Unseen Possibilities in Our Lives* (Woodstock, VT: Skylight Paths Publishing, 2003).

5. Lewis Richmond, *Aging as a Spiritual Practice: A Contemplative Guide to Growing Older and Wiser* (New York: Gotham Books, 2013).

6. Viktor Frankl, *Man's Search for Meaning* (Boston, MA: Beacon Press, 2006).

7. Robert Wright, *Why Buddhism Is True: The Science and Philosophy of Meditation and Enlightenment* (New York: Simon & Schuster, 2017).

8. "Exploring Your Spirituality After 60," The Esquiline Wellness Blog, accessed October 17, 2020, https://resources.theesquiline. org/blog/exploring-your-spirituality-after-60.

9. "Buddhism and Social Engagement," Ken Jones Zen (blog), accessed October 17, 2020, http://www.kenjoneszen.com/ buddhism-and-social-engagement.

XI

1. Bertrand Russell, *Portraits from Memory and Other Essays* (Los Angeles: James Press 2007).

Appendix B

_____

FURTHER RESOURCES WORTH YOUR ATTENTION

As we were researching, we acquired many books and articles. Here are a few we unreservedly recommend.

BOOKS

Cicero, Marcus Tullius. *How to Grow Old: Ancient Wisdom for the Second Half of Life*. Translated by Philip Freeman. Princeton, NJ: Princeton University Press, 2016.

> Don't let the "grow old" put you off. The subtitle promises "ancient wisdom for the second half of life," and Cicero delivers. A brief, accessible classic that should be required reading for everyone leaving middle age.

Klein, Daniel. *Travels with Epicurus: A Journey to a Greek Island in Search of a Fulfilled Life*. New York: Penguin Group, 2012.

> A brief, insightful narrative filled with gentle, sophisticated humor and wisdom about the search for happiness and meaning. We've given copies to our good friends.

Snowdon, David. *Aging with Grace: What the Nun Study Teaches Us About Leading Longer, Healthier, and More Meaningful Lives.* New York: Bantam Books, 2016.

> The fascinating results from a long-term study concerning nuns. It's filled with solid advice about living longer, heathier, and more meaningful lives. Certainly not just for Catholics or women!

Viorst, Judith. *Necessary Losses: The Loves, Illusions, Dependencies, and Impossible Expectations That All of Us Have to Give Up in Order to Grow.* New York: Simon & Schuster Paperbacks, 1986.

> Loss is a weighty but inescapable subject. The book is heavy going in some spots but really valuable reading. Think of it as essential preparation for the inevitable.

Smith, Hyrum W. *Purposeful Retirement: How to Bring Happiness and Meaning to Your Retirement.* Coral Gables, FL: Mango Publishing Group, 2017.

> By no means light reading but filled with keen observations and solid advice. The kind of book you mark up and keep going back to.

Ryan, Robin. *Retirement Reinvention: Make Your Next Act Your Best Act.* New York: Penguin Books, 2018.

> Plenty of good direction, helpful information, and solid advice from a professional retirement counselor.

Zelinski, Ernie. *How to Retire Happy, Wild, and Free.* Visions International Publishing, 2013.

An irreverent romp through the landscape of life after retiring. Plenty of good ideas, stories, and messages embedded in his schtick.

WEBSITES

Nextavenue.org

As far as we know, this is public media's first and only national journalism service for America's older population. Mission: to meet the needs, and unleash the potential, of older Americans through the power of media. Twin Cities Public TV runs it.

Retirement, https://www.forbes.com/sites/nextavenue/2018/04/01/21-unvarnished-truths-about-retirement/#4ae20d1f8e71.

Jonathan Look's edgy and insightful lessons from his early retirement.

Appendix C

POTENTIAL RETIREMENT ACTIVITIES

Here are activities that people told us work for them.

WORKING FOR MONEY

- Self-publish a book
- Become a part-time consultant
- Become a part-time or substitute teacher
- Become a part-time caregiver
- Become a worker or salesperson at a local retail store
- Buy and operate a small photography store
- Sell things on eBay
- Operate an Airbnb
- Work as a driver for Uber or Lyft
- Join a corporate board
- Arrange flowers for events
- Walk dogs
- Work as a library assistant

GIVING BACK

- Care for spouses, a significant other, parents, children, or grandchildren
- Take a position on a nonprofit board
- Become a mentor
- Become a tutor
- Become involved in giving to and/or working for charities, including hospital, church, and theater groups, as well as Habitat for Humanity, Meals on Wheels, and the Salvation Army
- Become involved in a political campaign
- Run for local office
- Work in an animal rescue/care operation
- Provide transportation to people who need assistance

TRAVEL

- On vacation, take buses and trains; drive
- Take cruises, which don't necessitate having to pack and unpack at every stop
- Visit national parks
- Travel nationally and internationally alone or with family and friends
- Visit friends and family
- Rent a room for a month or more in another city
- Spend time in warmer climates
- Participate in sports and travel objectives: kayak in fifty states, hike in certain parks, run or walk in marathons or other races, or visit golf courses
- Take a boat trip down the intercoastal waterway
- Travel to major nearby cities to see shows, museums, the symphony, an opera, or art galleries

EDUCATION

- Take a course, teach, or help manage schools
- Earn a high school, undergraduate, or graduate degree
- Help children and/or grandchildren with their education
- Attend or teach in a lecture series

Note: many public universities offer tuition-free classes for senior citizens https://www.thepennyhoarder.com/save-money/free-college-courses-for-senior-citizens/.

Note: internet education for retirees, https://www.nytimes.com/2015/03/20/education/free-online-courses-keep-retirees-in-the-know.html.

CREATIVE

- Paint pictures to give to family and friends
- Create pottery to give to family and friends
- Learn about photography and take photos for family and friends
- Write a book
- Write op-eds for local newspapers
- Write about personal experiences and/or an autobiography
- Create an oral history
- Start gardening
- Spend time building or renovating a home
- Play in a local orchestra or band
- Sing in a chorus or choir
- Join or start a group or club
- Play bridge, poker, mahjong, canasta, or other card games competitively or with friends
- Play card games on the internet with children and/or friends
- Join or start a book club

- Join or start an investment club
- Join with friends in regular breakfast, lunch, or dinner get-togethers

TAKE CARE OF YOUR BODY

- Do a health assessment
- Eat a balanced diet
- Work with a personal trainer to set up a workout program
- Determine a regular workout program that includes weights, balance, and cardiovascular exercises
- Find a place you like to work out
- Pick a time of day that works for you
- Join an exercise class
- Set up an exercise area in your home
- Consider what to do while working out: listen to music, read a book, listen to podcasts or audiobooks, or watch TV

TAKE CARE OF YOUR HEART

- Play sports: golf, tennis, fishing, hiking, biking, swimming, and kayaking
- Follow sports teams and attend sporting events
- Become involved in internet games and sports
- Take up line dancing or ballroom dancing
- Crew on a tall ship
- Coach or assistant coach a sports team

TAKE CARE OF YOUR BRAIN

- Maintain good social connections
- Limit time watching TV
- Limit time on the internet and social media

- Make sure you get enough sleep
- Do the daily puzzle, sudoku, or crossword
- Play bridge or chess
- Do arithmetic in your head rather than using a calculator
- Attend classes and lectures

TAKE CARE OF YOUR SOUL

- Spend time in nature
- Create art
- Serve others
- Learn and regularly practice yoga, tai chi, and meditation
- Work on mindfulness
- Attend weekly religious services
- Attend daily Mass
- Pray
- Practice giving yourself up to a superior being
- Spend more time on things you're thankful for
- Stay optimistic

ACKNOWLEDGMENTS

Writing a book is a challenge not to be taken lightly, particularly when the authors had done nothing remotely like it over their long careers. Fortunately, our choice of subject meant we had many sources who had made the transition from career to retirement. Their help was invaluable and came in two ways—helping us figure out how to convey what we'd learned and sharing our stories and insights.

We are particularly indebted to John Barstow, Elise Blair, Ed Knox, Stephen Donadio, Celia Cohen, Mark Gitenstein, Emmie Donadio, Fred Preiss, Dexter Hutchins, and Chuck Strum, whose coaching, encouragement, and expert counsel helped us at key junctures.

Without the benefit of so many friends and acquaintances willing to share their stories, our efforts might have produced only a sermon. Our particular thanks go to Cynthia Hewitt, Bart Dalton, Paul Fine, John Betz, Peter Caruthers, Nancy Ewen, Nick Causton, George Dorsey, Chuck Gibson, Charlie Grigg, Jack Goodman, John Graney, and Willard Jackson.

ABOUT THE AUTHORS

TED KAUFMAN is the former US Senator from Delaware succeeding Senator Joseph Biden. Ted was Biden's Chief of Staff for nineteen years and led his presidential transition planning in 2020. He taught at Duke Law School for twenty-six years. At eighty-one, he and his wife, Lynne, celebrate their sixty-first anniversary this year.

BRUCE HILAND'S career included McKinsey, more than five years as Chief Administrative Officer at Time Inc., twenty years of independent consulting, and four startups. Now eighty-one, he and Ginny, married fifty-seven years, are enjoying their family, dealing with aging, and harvesting the fruits of their labor.